MARX: A GUIDE FOR THE PERPLEXED

JOHN SEED

continuum

Continuum International Publishing Group

The Tower Building
11 York Road
London SE1 7NX

80 Maiden Lane
Suite 704
New York, NY 10038

www.continuumbooks.com

British Library Cataloguing-in-Publication Data
A catalogue record for this book is available from the British Library.

ISBN: HB: 978-0-8264-9334-7
PB: 978-0-8264-9335-4

Library of Congress Cataloging-in-Publication Data
Seed, John, 1950–
Marx : a guide for the perplexed / John Seed.
p. cm.
Includes bibliographical references (p.).
ISBN 978-0-8264-9334-7 -- ISBN 978-0-8264-9335-4
1. Marx, Karl, 1818–1883. I. Title.

B3305.M74S44 2010
335.4092--dc22

2010004491

Typeset by Newgen Imaging Systems Pvt Ltd, Chennai, India
Printed and bound in Great Britain by the MPG Books Group

CONTENTS

ABBREVIATIONS

MECW	*Collected Works of Marx and Engels*, 50 Vols, London: Lawrence & Wishart, 1975–2000
1971	*Marx and Engels. Articles on Britain*, Moscow: Progess Publishers, 1971
1973a	*Revolutions of 1848, Political Writings.* Vol. 1, ed. D. Fernbach, Harmondsworth: Penguin, 1973
1973b	*Surveys from Exile, Political Writings.* Vol. 2, ed. D. Fernbach, Harmondsworth: Penguin, 1973
1973c	*Grundrisse. Foundations of the Critique of Political Economy* (Rough Draft), trans. M. Nicolaus, Harmondsworth: Penguin, 1973
1974	*The First International and After, Political Writings.* Vol. 3, ed. D. Fernbach, Harmondsworth: Penguin, 1974
1975a	*Early Writings*, introduced by Lucio Colletti, trans R. Livingstone and G. Benton, Harmondsworth: Penguin, 1975
1975b	*Marx and Engels Selected Correspondence*, ed. S. W. Ryazanskaya, trans. I. Lasker, 3rd edition, Moscow: Progress Publishers, 1975
1976	*Capital. A Critique of Political Economy.* Vol. 1, intro. E. Mandel, trans. B. Fowkes, Harmondsworth: Penguin, 1976

1978	*Capital. A Critique of Political Economy.* Vol. 2, intro. E. Mandel, trans. D. Fernbach, Harmondsworth: Penguin, 1978
1981	*Capital. A Critique of Political Economy.* Vol. 3, intro. E. Mandel, trans. D. Fernbach, Harmondsworth: Penguin, 1981
2002	*The Communist Manifesto*, intro. G. Stedman Jones, Harmondsworth: Penguin, 2002
2007	*Dispatches from the New York Tribune: Selected Journalism of Karl Marx*, ed. J. Ledbetter, Harmondsworth: Penguin, 2007
2009	Friedrich Engels, *The Condition of the Working Class in England*, ed. V. Kiernan, intro. T. Hunt, Harmondsworth: Penguin, 2009

CHAPTER 1

INTRODUCTION: READING MARX

All social life is essentially practical. All mysteries which lead theory to mysticism find their rational solution in human practice and in the comprehension of that practice.

(*1975b: 423*)

Is there any nineteenth-century face as familiar as that of the bearded revolutionary sternly looking out of a Victorian London day and into the future from which we look back? By any scale of measurement, Karl Marx has been one of the most important intellectual figures of recent centuries, stimulating arguments across almost every intellectual discipline in every major language. Darwin and Freud are two other figures who have had a not dissimilar kind of impact. But neither of them was the inspiration for political movements which were to transform large parts of the globe in the twentieth century and to create states which proclaimed their commitment to his principles.

But this is where the problems begin. This is not a book about twentieth-century European politics or about the varieties of twentieth-century Marxism or about the Soviet Union. But it is impossible to read Marx without confronting a terrible and unfinished history. Any approach to Marx has to take some measure of his complex relations with Marxism, or rather, Marxism's relationship to Marx. Everyone knows his prescient quip: '*Ce qu'il y a de certain c'est que moi, je ne suis pas Marxiste.*'[1]

THE RUINS OF MARXISM

For much of the twentieth century the names 'Marx' or 'Marxism' immediately evoked the Soviet Union. The Russian

Revolution of 1917 created the first, and for many years the only state claiming to practice the principles of Marx. Since the point was not to interpret the world but to *change* it, Lenin and the Soviet Communist Party carried immense intellectual authority among Marxists world-wide. Early Marxist critics of the whole Soviet project, such as Karl Kautsky, Rosa Luxemburg, Julius Martov or Karl Korsch, were soon forgotten. The reach of Soviet Communism was massively extended in the aftermath of the Second World War. Large sections of Eastern Europe – eastern parts of Germany, Poland, Hungary, Czechoslovakia, Romania, Bulgaria and Yugoslavia – fell within the Soviet sphere of influence, as agreed at the Yalta and Potsdam conferences in 1945. Communist regimes were installed in the next few years. In 1949 the long civil war that had wracked China for a generation was brought to an end by the victory of the Communists. So by the early 1950s half of Europe and much of Asia stretched out under the red flag of Communism.

For several generations, Marx was merely the great forerunner of Lenin; Marxism became Marxism-Leninism. This was declared to be the only legitimate form of Marxism – Soviet Marxism – in a new doctrinal orthodoxy which disallowed alternative readings and thus their alternative and potentially subversive policy implications. But it also served the interests of those seeking to delegitimize *any* reading of Marx. If there was only the Marxist-Leninist reading then any appropriation of Marx was automatically contaminated by its association with the Soviet state – the supposed embodiment of Marx's political vision. Especially after 1956 and the revelations at the 20th Congress of the Soviet Communist Party, Marxism-Leninism now equalled Stalinism – and that signified purges, the gulag, forced labour, the secret police, barbed wire and a great deal of snow. The collapse of Soviet-style socialism in Russia and Eastern Europe in the early 1990s was final confirmation of the failure of Marxism-Leninism as a politics.

This kind of conclusion does not just come from the triumphalist political right. In his important study of the Australian Communist Party, Stuart MacIntyre states uncompromisingly: 'Communism is no more'. It ceased to exist with Gorbachev's *glasnost* and *perestroika*, the collapse of the people's democracies of Eastern Europe, the fall of the Berlin Wall, the disintegration of the Soviet Union and the dissolution of the Communist

Parties of the West. Communism, MacIntyre powerfully argues, collapsed under the weight of its own failures. Unable to respond to changing conditions of production and consumption it failed to meet many of the basic needs of its populations. As a form of thought Marxism-Leninism became lifeless, authoritarian, rigid and very very boring. As a form of government it became a monolithic one-party regime in which any spark of democracy, of innovation or initiative was snuffed out.[2] This point is complicated but confirmed by the remnants of Marxism-Leninism. Today the largest Communist state is, paradoxically, the largest capitalist economy on the planet – China. And it is flanked by two smaller Communist states – North Korea and Vietnam. In the Western hemisphere Communism is confined to the small Caribbean island of Cuba. There are no Communist Parties, much less Communist states in Europe and little likelihood of a revival of Marxist-Leninism.

Of course, Marxism was never the equivalent of Marxism-Leninism. In other parts of late nineteenth- and early twentieth-century Europe there were many other political forms which Marxism took – German social democracy, Council Communism, Austro-Marxism, for instance. These looked at the Soviet experiment, and the national Communist Parties which it engendered, with a sceptical eye. And there were sharp Marxist critiques of Soviet Marxist-Leninism from Rosa Luxemburg, from Gramsci and Trotsky in the 1930s, from Jean-Paul Sartre, Isaac Deutscher and Herbert Marcuse in the 1950s and 60s, among many others. It would be easy – too easy – to say that what failed in the Soviet Union and the Eastern bloc of socialist states was not Marxism, but a particular and aberrant variant – Soviet Marxism-Leninism. Indeed, it has been argued that the collapse of the Soviet Union vindicates not only the political scepticism of a long line of Marxist critics but also some of the core theses of the Marxist theory of history. After all, Marx had insisted that socialism was only possible on the basis of the full development of the forces of production under capitalism. As Erik Olin Wright has put it:

> The anomaly from the point of view of classical Marxism, therefore, is not that the state bureaucratic command economies have failed and are in a process of transition to capitalism, but that they survived for as long as they did.[3]

In a historical irony that any Marxist must glumly appreciate, it could be argued that the forces of production of the Soviet economy undermined its socialist relations of production and led to the revolutionary overthrow of the Soviet state. Much Marxist work in the 1970s went into analysing the transition from feudalism to capitalism and the transition from capitalism to socialism. Little attention was given to the transition from socialism to capitalism, an unexpected but considerably more important transition in global terms in the late twentieth century. Whether the new regimes of Russia, central Asia and Eastern Europe are triumphs of either capitalism or liberal democracy remains an open question. That the collapse of the Soviet Union has been a human catastrophe for millions of people living in its territories can hardly be doubted.[4]

As Louis Althusser remarked, 'the crisis of Marxism is not a recent phenomenon'. The history of Marxism has consisted of 'a long series of crises and transformations'. And this is as it should be, since this is precisely how history itself moves. The theory and practice of revolution can hardly be immune to crisis and transformation itself. But, whatever the value of Marxist interpretations of the collapse of the Soviet Union, they provide few comforts for the Marxist political project. Marx insisted on the significance of his work as a *political* intervention, as both a contribution to, and an expression of, revolutionary social change. History seems to have taken another direction. In the words of Schiller: '*Die Weltgeschichte ist das Weltgericht*' – 'World History is the World's Court'. Marx said something similar himself, at the end of a short speech to English Chartists in 1856: 'History is the judge – its executioner, the proletarian'. History's judgement on Marxism is hardly very positive. It is not only the Marxism-Leninism of the Soviet Union and its satellites which has disintegrated in recent decades. Over a century after Marx's death working-class organizations committed to some form of socialism, in Europe at least, have rarely been at such a low ebb. In Italy, once the flagship of a new and adventurous form of Marxist politics, Eurocommunism, the organized left has more or less disintegrated. The Italian Communist Party, which got over 34 per cent of the vote in the 1976 general election, split in 1991 and its fragments went into rapid decline. *L'Unita*, the former Italian Communist Party newspaper, selling 250,000 copies each day in the 1970s closed down in 2000. Its sales had dropped to 50,000 as the socialist culture of the post-war period faded away. The French Communist Party survives, but only as a shadow of the major political party it once was. From the 1930s to the 1970s its percentage of votes in elections for the French National Assembly was between 20 per cent and 30 per cent. During the 1980s and 90s the figure fell to around 10 per cent and in the last two general elections has been less than 5 per cent.[5]

And the same picture emerges across Western Europe – political parties of the left weak and profoundly compromised, trade union membership in decline. A generation ago the Labour Party in Britain was a broad church for all kinds of socialists, radicals, reformers and even Marxists of one kind or another. Labour governments were never as radical or as socialist as many of its members but no Labour Government ever abased itself before the short-term interests of multinational corporations and the foreign policy of the most right-wing Washington government in generations, in the way that Tony Blair and Gordon Brown did after 2001. With members resigning in droves during the last decade, party branches ceasing to exist in many parts of the country or limping along with a handful of members, the Labour Party survives as an empty hulk, an organization dedicated to the careers and the expense accounts of professional politicians and image consultants. No political organization of the left has developed to take its place, despite massive waves of political alienation and bitter discontent.

As Eric Hobsbawm commented in his influential history of the twentieth century: 'if Marx would live on as a major thinker, which could hardly be doubted, none of the versions of Marxism formulated since the 1890s as doctrines of political action and aspiration for socialist movements were likely to do so in their original forms.'[6] However, as Hobsbawm went on to note, the counter-utopia of free market capitalism was equally bankrupt. Coming from an old Marxist these comments might be ascribed more to hope than reality. But in a remarkable and unexpected intervention in the aftermath of the fall of Communism, Jacques Derrida, the doyen of post-structuralism, wrote in similar terms, both about the continuing significance of Marx and about the overhasty celebrations of a new thousand-year Reich of free-market capitalism: 'To the rhythm of a cadenced march, it proclaims: Marx is dead, communism is dead, very dead, and along with it its hopes, its discourses, its theories, and its practices.' For a while it was seriously argued that liberal free-market capitalism was the 'end point of mankind's ideological evolution', the 'final form of human government', 'the end of history'. But, Derrida went on, this 'manic triumphalism' is so loud and insistent precisely because it is trying to drown out the bitter truth: 'never in history, has the horizon of the thing whose survival is being celebrated (namely all the old models of the capitalist and liberal world) been as dark, threatening and threatened'.[7] It will always be a mistake not to reread Marx and now that what he called 'the dogma machine' of Marxist state apparatuses had collapsed, there is even less excuse for not reading Marx. There will be no future without Marx, 'without the memory and inheritance of Marx', according to Derrida.

The communism inspired by Lenin and the Russian revolution has gone, but Marx is still here. And so is the bankruptcy of actually existing capitalism; quite literally: after lurching through several crises, the whole international financial system cracked down the middle in the autumn of 2008 and the global economy teetered on the brink of collapse. Now in the spring and summer of 2009 the world is falling into the deepest economic crisis in seventy years. Unemployment is spiralling upwards in every capitalist economy. At the same time, sales of *The Communist Manifesto* have skyrocketed: Amazon.com reporting a 700 per cent increase since the banking collapse.[8] In Berlin, copies of Marx's *Capital* were reported to have sold out as sales increased from around 100 a year to more to more than 2,500 copies in the first ten months of 2008. And Marx appeared on the cover of the European edition of *Time Magazine* in 2 February 2009.[9] A spectre is haunting the new century which seems to be a world of incessant war in which so-called free trade and globalization have enriched a minority, leaving tens of millions in deteriorating conditions, working longer hours for a declining real income in a gigantic global sweatshop.

This is not a book about the future of socialism, about anti-capitalism and anti-globalization. Nor is it a study of twentieth-century Marxism and its continuing impact on contemporary political debate or its influence on current academic work across the Humanities and Social Sciences. Though written in the light of these contexts, its focus is more precise: to return to the texts of Marx and to explore ways of making sense of them.

READING WHAT?

This brings us to another question. When we say, 'Marx', what are we trying to understand? What does the name 'Karl Marx' designate? What are we reading? The simplest answer is a body of writing which has the name Karl Marx attached as its author. But this body of writing is large, complex and inconsistent. The published *oeuvre* of Karl Marx today consists of a few major studies which he completed and saw through the press himself, notably the first volume of *Capital.* But it also includes many texts that were co-authored with Friedrich Engels. And many of the texts that carry the name 'Karl Marx' were never completed by him, and often never intended for publication. So any reading of Marx has to begin with the complex character of the texts that bear his name.

Capital was his great project for at least the last 30 years of his life, but only the first volume was completed and published under his direct supervision. Its later publication history is complicated. Marx himself made revisions for the second German edition of volume one of *Capital*, published in 1872. He also provided suggestions for the Russian translation of the same volume, published in St Petersburg in the same year. He then introduced further revisions to the French translation, appearing in serial form from 1872. Engels edited a third German edition in 1883, incorporating Marx's changes from the French edition of 1873. This third German edition was the source for the English translation of volume one of *Capital,* published in 1887. No sequel to this first volume of *Capital* was completed by Marx. What remained were huge quantities of manuscript material in various states of completion. Engels, one of the very few people who could decipher Marx's handwriting, set to work on putting this material into some kind of publishable form. Volume two of *Capital*, drafted by Marx at various times between 1863 and 1878, appeared in 1885 – a revised second edition appeared in 1893. And volume three of *Capital*, drafted by Marx between 1863 and his death in 1883, was published in 1894. As Engels admitted in his preface to the first edition of the former:

> It was no easy task to put the second book of *Capital* in shape for publication, and do it in a way that on the one hand would make it a connected and as far as possible complete work, and

> on the other would represent exclusively the work of its author, not of its editor.

And he proceeded to itemize and carefully describe the huge amounts of manuscript material which he had shaped into this volume and which would be further reshaped for further volumes.

Capital was not the only work of Marx assembled from his manuscripts after his death. A number working drafts, notebooks and manuscripts, from every stage of his career, were published posthumously. Perhaps the two most important works of his early period were never finished. *The Economic and Philosophical Manuscripts of 1844*, sometimes known as *The Paris Manuscripts*, was left as a series of draft chapters in 1844. Parts of it were lost. What survived was first published in Moscow in 1932 in the German edition of the collected works of Marx and Engels. The first English translation appeared in 1959. Perhaps the most important of the works of the 1840s was *The German Ideology*. Co-authored with Engels between September 1845 and the summer of 1846, it never found a publisher. The huge manuscript was left, as Marx put it, to 'the gnawing criticism of the mice'. Several chapters have disappeared. A few parts were published in Germany before 1914. Chapter I, 'Feuerbach', perhaps the most important chapter, was published in Moscow in a Russian translation in 1924 and in German in 1926. The whole work was finally published in German in Moscow in 1932. Editions and selections only appeared in English in the 1960s.[10]

The most important material from Marx's middle period is the *Grundrisse*, so called from the first word of the German title: *Grundrisse der Kritik der politschen Oekonomie* ('Outlines of a Critique of Political Economy'). It consists of seven notebooks drafted by Marx during the winter of 1857–8. This was another substantial piece of work, adding up to more than 800 pages of closely printed text. A limited edition was published in Moscow in two volumes, in 1939 and 1941, under the editorship of the Marx-Engels-Lenin Institute, Moscow, but few copies of this edition ever reached western Europe. It was reissued in a single volume in Berlin in 1953. A few sections were later published in English but the whole text only finally appeared in English in 1973.

Alongside his published works of theory, notably *Capital*, Marx's *oeuvre* also includes a variety of political writings. Some of these – such as the *Eighteenth Brumaire of Louis Bonaparte* – are substantial and sophisticated works of analysis. But some of them are occasional pieces – addresses, public letters, printed speeches and reports – written in very specific political circumstances. In addition to these kinds of occasional political writing there is Marx's vast output of journalism, which includes around 700 articles written for German and American newspapers between 1842 and 1862.

Finally, there is the question of Engels. It was his money which supported the Marx family for years, but he was also closely involved in everything that Marx wrote from 1844. He provided information on the cotton industry, he debated every issue that Marx was exploring and he commented on his writing, before and after publication. For instance, Engels read the drafts and proofs of *Capital* at every stage. When the huge first volume was finally ready for printing Marx wrote to Engels:

> So this volume is finished. It was thanks to you alone that this became possible. Without your self-sacrifice for me I could never possibly have done the enormous work for the three volumes. I embrace you, full of thanks. (1975b: 180)

Engels continued to play a crucial role in the posthumous editing and dissemination of Marx's works. There were new editions of the *Communist Manifesto*: in German (1883, 1890), Russian (1882), English (1888), Polish (1892) and Italian (1893). And a series of important writings by Marx dating from the 1840s and 50s were reprinted in these years, including *The Poverty of Philosophy, Wage-Labor and Capital, The Communist Trial in Cologne* and *The Class Struggles in France.* In all of these Engels had a significant hand, frequently contributing prefaces and editorial notes, even revising the text.[11] Engels not only edited and published long-forgotten texts by Marx. He also produced many of his own and some of these soon found a wider readership than anything written by Marx. His *Anti-Duhring*, in particular, was read as a definitive statement of Marx's doctrine by several generations of European socialists. A polemic against a now-forgotten figure, it became a canonical text of 'Marxism'. Three key chapters were turned into the pamphlet *Socialism, Utopian and Scientific* which circulated in numerous editions and translations.

For some commentators, Engels was the willing subordinate of Marx. Their views were taken to be virtually identical. Engels therefore did valuable work in popularizing Marx's views, making them accessible to socialists everywhere, in a way that *Capital* never could. This was very much the view of leading thinkers of German social democracy, and of the Second International, many of whom – such as Kautsky, Bernstein, Liebknecht and Bebel – were under the direct personal influence of Engels. And it was this first generation of European disciples of Engels who formulated what was to become the new Marxism of the years before 1914. They had *Capital* and they had several philosophical texts produced by Engels in the 1870s and 1880s. They also tended to share a common cultural formation in which Darwin, and certain forms of scientific and positivist thinking were in the ascendency. At the very graveside of Marx, Engels had affiliated the work of Marx to that of Darwin.

For Soviet orthodoxy too, Marx and Engels were joint authors of a single body of work. This is signalled in the very title of the Marx-Engels Institute in Moscow, where Engels is represented alongside Marx (though not in alphabetical order) as founding father of Marxism-Leninism. For a line of thinkers in Western Marxism, however, the balance sheet is more complex. Engels, it is argued, made important early contributions to the development of Marx's thought. However, he lacked philosophical subtlety and was responsible for introducing a degree of positivism and scientism into Marxism, pointing forward to the crude scientism of Soviet dialectical materialism. So, the argument goes, it was not Marx but Engels who created 'Marxism' and who was really the father of the dialectical and historical materialism that became 'Marxism-Leninism' and the basis of official philosophy in the Soviet Union.[12]

VOICES

Returning to Marx's *oeuvre*, how then can we make sense of this large and complicated body of writings? These texts bearing the name 'Karl Marx' include very different kinds of writing – finished works of social and economic theory, substantial journal articles, brief newspaper articles, political speeches, rough drafts of work in progress, even private letters – and works co-authored in one way or another with Engels. And they were produced during more than 40 years of intellectual and political activity in Germany, France, Belgium and England. It is hardly surprising that this collection of writings bearing the name 'Karl Marx' is fragmentary, discrepant and full of inconsistencies. And it is worth remembering the sheer size of Marx's project. The first volume of *Capital* consists of over 900 pages. The posthumous second and third volumes of *Capital* add a further 1,500 pages of print. Further drafts of *Capital*, subsequently assembled as *Theories of Surplus Value*, add up to another three large volumes and nearly 2,000 pages in German. Marx didn't publish a great deal in his later years but he wrote constantly and on a massive scale. To understand this enormous and complicated body of work is a forbidding task and any attempt is bound to omit some significant aspects. However, it is better to discuss Marx too briefly than not at all.

Marx: A Guide for the Perplexed does its limited best to focus on what Marx himself prioritized. First, there are his analyses of the workings of the capitalist system through a critical engagement with political economy – the *Grundrisse* and *Capital* are the key texts here. Second, there are his attempts to understand contemporary politics through close analysis of contemporary events. *The Class Struggles in France* and the *Eighteenth Brumaire* are probably the two most important works here – but there are a number of important shorter newspaper articles from the 1840s and 50s which are also valuable. Third, there are Marx's practical political interventions to guide the political strategy of organized labour – *Critique of Gotha Programme* and various writings from the 1860s and 1870s associated with International Working Man's Association, for instance. These are not cut-and-dried categories of writing: several works fit into more than one. Indeed, it is one of the arguments of this book that in one way or another virtually everything Marx wrote was a political intervention. At the same time even Marx's very specific political writings are characterized by a commitment to theoretical understanding.

By concentrating on what Marx himself prioritized, necessarily some important contemporary issues do not figure in the pages that follow. The most important of these is the question of gender and sexuality. This has been a major issue both inside the academy and in everyday social and political life, especially since the 1970s, through the impact of feminism and the women's movement. Marx was not entirely oblivious of questions surrounding gender and the family. They were raised by the utopian socialists in Britain, France and elsewhere in the 1830s and 1840s. *The German Ideology* showed some interest in questions to do with biological reproduction and the history of the family. *The Communist Manifesto* kept open some channels of communication to utopian socialism, attacking bourgeois marriage and the bourgeois family as ideals which had little reality for the working class – and anyway amounted to little more than legalized prostitution (2002: 239–40). These questions seem to have been put on one side by Marx after 1848 as he concentrated his attention on his critique of political economy and on economic and social structures which, it might be argued, affected working-class men and women (and children) in largely similar ways.[13] In the pages of *Capital* 'the motley crowd of labourers' whose experiences are so richly represented in official reports are, Marx says, 'of all callings, ages, sexes'. Different groups of workers – male or female, English, Irish or Scottish, white or black, old or young – are vulnerable to different forms of coercion, but they are equally subjected to the despotism of capital in the workplace and the insecurity of the labour market. If *Capital* did not explore the specificity of women's oppression under capitalism, it did set out a series of conceptual frameworks which could be utilized to that end – as in the important debate of the 1970s around domestic labour.[14] The question of the family and the position of women resurfaced in Engels book *The Origins of the Family*, partly based on Marx's late anthropological studies. This has been an influential if controversial work among feminists.[15] It also influenced not just Marxist writings in subsequent decades by such as August Bebel, Klara Zetkin and Alexandra Kollantai, but also the policies of Communist states.

Another major issue which I have not attended to is the question of art and high culture. Marx was remarkably well read in several languages – as Siegbert Prawer has documented – and his writings are studded with literary references.[16] He read to his daughters the whole of Homer, the *Niebelungen Lied*, *Don Quixote*, and *The Arabian Nights*. 'As to Shakespeare', Eleanor recalled in 1895, 'he was the Bible of our house, seldom out of our hands or mouths. By the time I was six I knew scene upon scene of Shakespeare by heart'. And over the next few years she and Marx read together novels, most of the novels of Fennimore Cooper, Sir Walter Scott, Henry Fielding and Balzac.

> And while he talked about these and many other books he would, all unconscious though she was of it, show his little girl where to look for all that was finest and best in the works, teach

her – though she never thought she was being taught, to that she would have objected – to try and think, to try and understand for herself.[17]

According to his son-in-law, Paul Lafargue: 'He admired Balzac so much that he wished to write a review of his great work *La Comedie Humaine* as soon as he had finished his book on economics.' For Marx, through this series of novels Balzac was 'the historian of his time'. However, there is no coherent or systematic theory of art to be found in the writings of Marx. Twentieth-century Marxism has more than made up for this and questions of art and culture have occupied much more attention among Marxists in western Europe and North America than Marx's own preoccupations.[18] No doubt there are other important topics which Marx's work may be utilized to explore further – Marx and science, Marx and ecology, Marx and international relations and so on.

In *Marx: A Guide for the Perplexed* I have chosen to pursue a reading of some of the central texts of Marx chronologically as well as thematically: the development of his political thinking in the 1840s, culminating in the *Communist Manifesto* and his active involvement in the revolutions of 1848; his rethinking of some of the theoretical positions carved out in the 1840s and his increasing engagement with political economy in the course of the 1850s; the critique of political economy elaborated in the first volume of *Capital*; the politics of labour that followed from this critique in the 1860s; and his interventions of the 1870s in politics in France, Germany and Russia. Each of these occupies a chapter and is discussed through close readings of key texts by Marx.

A final comment: this book is not, I want to stress, another attempt to manufacture yet one more final interpretation of Marx. Instead, I try to indicate how different and equally productive readings are often possible. In this I believe it is true to the essence of Marx's own critical project. In a suggestive brief essay, 'Marx's Three Voices', Maurice Blanchot pointed to the openness and heterogeneity of Marx's writings. He identified three distinct 'voices' – the philosophical, the political and the scientific. The first rehearses at length, without coming to any certain answers, traditional philosophical questions about history and alienation and man. The second voice, by contrast, is brief, urgent and to the point: 'It no longer carries a meaning but a call, a violence, a decision of rupture'.

The third is the indirect speech of scientific discourse. For Blanchot the voice of writing, as exemplified by Marx, is 'a voice of ceaseless contestation' and one that must break itself into multiple forms. 'The communist voice is always *at once* tacit and violent, political and scholarly, direct, indirect, total and fragmentary, lengthy and almost instantaneous'. The heterogeneity of Marx's texts thus destabilizes the position of the reader who must constantly submit himself, or herself, to revision and re-reading.[19] I am conscious, therefore, that this book is itself unfinished and unfinishable – like everything written about Marx. Its aim is to provide ways *into* the writings of Marx. It is an *introduction*, not a conclusion.

CHAPTER 2

POLITICS: THE 1848 REVOLUTIONS

Where speculation ends – in real life – there real, positive science begins: the representation of the practical activity, of the practical process of development of men. Empty talk about consciousness ceases, and real knowledge has to take its place.

(MECW5: 37)

'The philosophers have only *interpreted* the world in various ways; the point is to *change* it' (1975a:423). The young Marx said so in 1845 in one of his more famous pronouncements. Politics was not simply something that Marx took an interest in – one department of his thinking. It was integral to virtually everything he did and wrote. 'Marx was before all else a revolutionist', as Engels said at his funeral: 'His real mission in life was to contribute, in one way or another, to the overthrow of capitalist society and of the state institutions which it had brought into being . . .' (MECW24: 467–8).

In the years immediately preceding the *Communist Manifesto* and the revolutions of 1848, the young Karl Marx was locked in an intense critical engagement and an extended polemic with a series of influential contemporary thinkers' works in Germany, France and England. His critical responses to Hegel and the young Hegelians, to the political language inherited from the French Revolution, to various socialist writers such as Proudhon and to the British political economists were important and require discussion. It concedes too much to ideas, however, to suggest that Marx's evolving political understanding was solely a matter of critical thinking about particular political texts or to take Marx as some kind of genteel scholar interested in elaborating a political philosophy in polite dialogue with Aristotle, Locke, Hobbes or Hegel. Marx also learned the futility of liberal politics through bitter experience in the Germany of the 1840s. His political thinking is inseparable from his political activities and inseparable therefore from the political realities of nineteenth-century Britain, Europe and the wider world. Chapters 5 and 6 will examine the political thinking (and practice) of Marx during the later years of exile in London. In this chapter the focus is on Marx's political formation in the 1840s, on the *Communist Manifesto* of 1848 (perhaps the most influential text he ever wrote), and on his political experiences during the German revolution of 1848–9.

PRUSSIA

Karl Marx was born in 1818 in Trier, in the Prussian Rhineland, the son of Heinrich Marx, a prosperous Jewish lawyer. There were many generations of rabbis on both sides of his family, but his father had embraced with enthusiasm the ideals of the French Enlightenment and at the age of 35, for political reasons, had himself baptized into the Lutheran Church. Marx was brought up in a cultured and liberal household, surrounded by books and art, by generous parents and doting sisters. He studied for a year at the University of Bonn and then at the University of Berlin. But he was already running into trouble with the Prussian authorities. His doctoral thesis of 1841, on Ancient Greek philosophy, was not submitted to Berlin, where his association with radical intellectuals had cast a shadow over his academic future. Instead his doctorate was awarded, *in absentia*, by the University of Jena, outside the jurisdiction of Prussia.

For young reformers like Marx, excluded from academic positions or, like Marx's teacher Bauer, dismissed from their posts, crusading journalism offered a way of engaging in politics. In 1842 Marx became a contributor and then editor of the *Rheinische Zeitung*, a reforming newspaper set up by a group of middle-class liberals in Cologne, This brought Marx into direct and daily contact with contemporary issues. He was forced to deal with practical questions – about the rights of poor peasants to collect firewood or the impoverished conditions of local wine-growers, for instance. As he recalled in 1859:

> In the year 1842–43, as editor of the *Rheinische Zeitung,* I first found myself in the embarrassing position of having to discuss

> what is known as material interests. The deliberations of the Rhenish Landtag on forest thefts and the division of landed property; the official polemic started by Herr von Schaper, then Oberprasident of the Rhine Province, against the *Rheinische Zeitung* about the condition of the Moselle peasantry, and finally the debates on free trade and protective tariffs caused me in the first instance to turn my attention to economic questions. (1975a: 424)

From the start Marx's newspaper was in trouble with the Prussian authorities and after five months of wearying conflict he resigned as editor. The newspaper was closed by the government a few weeks later. The censorship and eventual closure of the *Rheinische Zeitung* made it obvious that the Prussian state represented partial and powerful economic interests and that it used its power to silence and control other sections of society. The power of the Prussian state, and the interests it represented, made it equally obvious to the 25-year-old Marx that philosophical criticism was powerless to do much to remedy this situation; indeed at its worst it was a frivolous distraction.

What kind of reforming politics was feasible in Germany in 1843? Patient conformity to the Prussian regime in the hopes of possible change at some future date was not acceptable to Marx. He told the liberal reformer Arnold Ruge that, 'stifled' in the atmosphere of censorship and surveillance, the closing down of his paper was a kind of liberation:

> It is a bad thing to have to perform menial duties even for the sake of freedom; to fight with pinpricks, instead of with clubs. I have become tired of hypocrisy, stupidity, gross arbitrariness, and of our bowing and scraping, dodging, and hair-splitting over words. Consequently, the government has given me back my freedom . . . I can do nothing more in Germany. (MECW1: 397–8)

A point he reiterated a few weeks later: 'it is impossible for me to write under Prussian censorship or to live in the Prussian atmosphere'. Travelling into political exile on a canal-boat, he voiced the shame which he and other Germans felt about 'the disgusting despotism' of the Prussian system. And he added some baleful comments on 'the impending revolution' and the fate of the Prussian king, summoning the ghosts of the executed Charles I and Louis XVI : 'The comedy of despotism that is being played out with us is just as dangerous for him, as the tragedy once was for the Stuarts and Bourbons' (MECW3: 133–4).

In Paris from October 1843, Marx's found himself at the centre of an international community of revolutionary intellectuals. Here he became a fully fledged communist, finding in the class-conscious and often revolutionary French workers a political agency for change. There is a revealing moment in one of his manuscripts at this time when he talks of how French socialist workers, gathering together for political purposes, prefigure the sociability of the future: 'Company, association, conversation, which in its turn has society as its goal, is enough for them. The brotherhood of man is not a hollow phrase, it is a reality, and the nobility of man shines forth upon us from their work-worn figures' (1975a: 365). It sounds as if Marx had witnessed – and been moved by – such gatherings. In Paris Marx resumed his career as a reforming journalist, co-editing with Ruge the *Deutsche-Französische Jahrbücher.* Appearing in French and German, this periodical proposed to build intellectual exchanges between the two countries and was committed to a radical political programme. A single issue appeared in April 1844 before once again the Prussian government intervened. Copies were seized and an arrest warrant issued against its editors on grounds of high treason. Shortly afterwards Marx was expelled from France at the behest of the Prussian authorities. He was allowed to settle in Brussels only on condition that he publishes nothing on contemporary politics.

Through his experiences as a student, as an aspirant academic and then as a young reforming journalist Marx had confronted the repressive character of the Prussian state and had learned the futility of opposing reality with concepts. As he commented in *The Holy Family*, drafted in the autumn of 1844: '*Ideas* can never lead beyond an old world order but only beyond the ideas of the old world order. Ideas *cannot carry out anything* at all. In order to carry out ideas men are needed who can exert practical force' (MECW4: 118). This was part of a critique of one of his old radical teachers, Bruno Bauer, and part of an argument about the French Revolution. It represents something of Marx's new and hard-won passage from philosophical speculation to political reality.

But where were these men capable of exerting 'practical force' to be found?

PHILOSOPHY AND REVOLUTION

Probably no period of Marx's intellectual labour was so intensive as the years 1843–6 during which he engaged critically with a series of the most advanced thinkers in German philosophy, in French politics and in British political economy. In a sense, the whole of his theory was generated out of a remarkable course of critical reading and thinking and polemic in these years. No wonder then, that more has been written about this remarkable moment of critique and synthesis in the mid-1840s than about the rest of his work. Three dimensions of the complex development of Marx's political thinking are worth pointing to here: first, his critiques of Hegel and the young Hegelians, who were in the ascendant in Germany; second, his explorations of the history of the French Revolution and variants of the French revolutionary tradition; and third, his studies of some of the key texts of British political economy.

'A Contribution to the Critique of Hegel's Philosophy of Right', published in the single issue of the *Deutsch-Französische Jahrbücher* in February, 1844, is an important expression of Marx's thinking at this juncture. It includes one of his most famous remarks – that religion is 'the opium of the people'. This was part of a much subtler and more complex argument. Religion is like an opiate not merely because it induces fantasy but because its function is to dull the pain of existence. It provides, Marx says, 'consolation and justification': 'Religious suffering is, at one and the same time, the expression of real suffering and a protest against real suffering. Religion is the sigh of the oppressed creature, the heart of a heartless world, and the soul of soulless conditions' (1975a: 244). Religion provides an *illusory* happiness. To call for the abolition of that illusory happiness is, Marx goes on, to demand *real* happiness: 'To call on them to give up their illusions about their condition is to call on them to give up a condition that requires illusions.' The critique of religion, therefore, points to a broader criticism of a world in which religion is necessary, or possible. It arouses people from their dreams and illusions but not in order to live without hope in a cold, grey, heartless world but, on the contrary, to realize the dreams of religion in *this* world. To abolish religion and its world of illusions requires the practical abolition of all the conditions of life which sustain religion. Thus, Marx says, 'the criticism of heaven turns into the criticism of the earth' (1975a: 244). The focus of critique switches from religion and theology to law and politics. And it moves beyond theory to revolutionary practice and 'the *categorical imperative to overthrow all relations* in which man is a debased, enslaved forsaken, despicable being . . .'.

'A Contribution to the Critique of Hegel's Philosophy of Right' also voices Marx's anger at the backwardness of Germany. The present German regime is, he says, an 'anachronism': 'We have shared the restorations of modern nations without ever having shared their revolutions' (1975a: 245). But German political backwardness has had the odd effect of generating in compensation an advanced philosophy in Kant, Hegel and a host of lesser philosophers: 'We are the *philosophical* contemporaries of the present without being its *historical* contemporaries . . . What for advanced nations is a *practical* quarrel with modern political conditions is for Germany, where such conditions do not yet exist, a *critical* quarrel with their reflection in philosophy' (1975a: 249). In other words, in politics the Germans *thought* what other nations *did*. In this situation, paradoxically, a critique of German philosophy was at the radical cutting edge of political *thinking*. But where is the political *practice*? Where is the group that can meet this advanced philosophy, wake Germany out of its dream-history and transform the political reality which sustains it? Marx grumbles about the mediocrity, the petty egoism of different social groups in Germany, none of which, he says, has 'the constituency, the penetration, the courage, or the ruthlessness that could mark it out as the negative representative of society'. There is only one negation of these dreary German realities:

> [A] class with *radical chains*, a class of civil society which is not a class of civil society, a class which is the dissolution of all classes, a sphere which has a universal character because of its universal suffering and which lays claims to no *particular right* because the wrong it suffers is not a *particular wrong*, but *wrong in general*, . . . which is, in a word, the *total loss* of humanity and which therefore can redeem itself only through the *total redemption of humanity*. This dissolution of society as a particular class is the *proletariat*. (1975a: 256)

The working class, the proletariat, has no particular grievances or interests. It is not one among a number of squabbling groups. Without a voice, without rights or representation of any kind, it was the negation of all existing social groups. This is Marx's first use of the term 'proletariat' and its role as the agent of revolutionary change.[1] But at this point he is still writing in very abstract terms about 'negation' and 'true democracy'. There were a few concrete proposals in this critique of Hegelian political philosophy – abolition of the monarchy, universal suffrage – but there is little empirical analysis of the 'radical chains' of the proletariat or the political strategies required to break them.

THE FRENCH REVOLUTION

Critical thinking about the French Revolution was a second key element of Marx's political formation in the 1840s. From the summer of 1843 Marx began an intensive course of reading on the French Revolution about which he was intending to write some kind of history. It was never written, but his thinking about the events in France of half a century before appeared in several of his writings at this time – and throughout his later work. 'On the Jewish Question', a critique of Marx's old radical teacher Bruno Bauer, included a careful examination, and critique, of the political language of the revolution and the bourgeois liberalism which emerged from it. The post-1789 French Constitution laid down 'the natural and imprescriptible rights of man' as equality, liberty, security and property. Liberty is specified as the right to do everything that harms no one else. It is, above all, the right of a man to enjoy his property. Equality and security are similarly concerned with the individual and his property rights. But, Marx comments, this kind of political language is anti-social. It lacks any understanding of the tissue of social relations through which the lives of actual men and women are shaped in everyday-life. It represents 'man' as 'an isolated monad, withdrawn into himself' and separated from other men: 'It makes every man see in other men not the realization of his own freedom, but the *barrier* to it':

> [N]ot one of the so-called rights of man goes beyond egoistic man, man as a member of civil society, namely as an individual withdrawn into himself, his private interest and his private

> desires and separated from the community . . . The only bond which holds them together is natural necessity, need and private interest, the conservation of their property and their egoistic persons. (1975a: 230)

On the one hand, through the revolutionary transformations of 1789 to 1794 men were freed from the politicization of private life in the form of the estates, corporations, guilds, and privileges of *ancien regime* France. But the corollary of this depoliticization of civil society – 'the world of needs, of labour, of private interests and of civil law' – was the ascendency of individualism in everyday life. From this perspective, it was only 'economic man', the private person locked in the struggles of the world of material interests, who possesses real, concrete existence.

The state, on the other hand was the sphere of an abstract and ideal universality, disconnected from 'civil society'. As a political subject, a citizen, he belonged to a political community which existed only as an abstraction: '*political* man is simply abstract, artificial man, man as an allegorical, moral person'. The fictitious equality and fellowship of this idealized political world disguised and in some ways redeemed the inequality, poverty and conflict of real life. There is a parallel here with Marx's critique of religion: the state is to civil society as heaven is to earth. 'Man in his immediate reality, in civil society, is a profane being. In the state, on the other hand, he is the imaginary member of a fictitious sovereignty, he is divested of his real individual life and filled with an unreal universality' (1975a: 220). Like the Christian heaven, the bourgeois liberal state represents an ideal sphere – one that realizes human needs that remain unrealized in the profane or material world, the real world of civil society. As Marx succinctly put it: 'the completion of the idealism of the state was at the same time the completion of the materialism of civil society'. Men are bifurcated into an isolated, self-seeking and anti-social individual in civil society on the one hand and an ideal juridical person, a citizen, on the other. Marx contrasts the kind of narrowly *political* emancipation that followed 1789 with *human* emancipation. The latter, he suggests, must provide a new kind of social integration of civil society and the state, of the citizen and the private individual:

> Only when real, individual man resumes the abstract citizen into himself and as an individual man has become a *species-being*

> in his empirical life, his individual work and in his individual relationships, only when man has recognized and organized his *forces propres* as *social forces* so that social force is no longer separated from him in the form of *political* force, only then will human emancipation be completed. (1975a: 234)

Again the critique is couched in abstract antitheses.

For Marx, one of the enduring political lessons of the fate of the Jacobins of 1793 was that no matter how revolutionary the political will, it was doomed to failure unless economic and social conditions made its aims practical. In *The Holy Family* in 1845 he came back to the discrepancy between political rhetoric and social reality in the French Revolution, speaking movingly of the political delusions of ill-fated Jacobins such as Saint-Just. After the fall of Robespierre, the powerful language of the rights of man found its unheroic realization in the acquisitiveness of modern bourgeois society. Freed by the revolution and the reign of terror from 'the trammels of feudalism', a new bourgeois society emerged with the Directory in 1795: 'A storm and stress of commercial enterprise, a passion for enrichment, the exuberance of the new bourgeois life, whose first self-enjoyment is pert, light-hearted, frivolous and intoxicating . . .' (MECW4: 122–3). This Marx said, was the '*real* enlightenment of the *land* of France'. Jacobins like Saint-Just could never understand that the great ideals of the rights of man, for which they fought and often died, were realized in such banal and trivial realities.

This was one of the central foundations of Marx's political thinking for the remainder of his life. If men wish to create a new social reality, he argued in a polemic of 1847, 'they first have to *produce* the *material conditions* of a new society itself, and no exertion of mind or will can free them from this fate.' In other words, political power of itself is insufficient to create a new social order. As the French Revolution had demonstrated, revolutionary popular political action only furthered the rule of capital, unless economic and social conditions were ripe for communism:

> If . . . the proletariat overthrows the political rule of the bourgeoisie, its victory will only be temporary, only an element in the service of the *bourgeois revolution* itself, as in the year 1794, as long as in the course of history, in its 'movement', the material

> conditions have not yet been created which make necessary the abolition of the bourgeois mode of production and therefore also the definitive overthrow of the political rule of the bourgeoisie. The terror in France could thus by its mighty hammer-blows only serve to spirit away, as it were, the ruins of feudalism from French soil. The timidly considerate bourgeoisie would not have accomplished this task in decades. The bloody action of the people thus only prepared the way for it. (MECW6: 312ff.)

The political experience of the Jacobins and the sans-culottes was both a major resource and a tragic lesson for Marx.

ENGELS AND POLITICAL ECONOMY

While Marx was engaging in a critical dialogue with the French revolutionary tradition in Paris, another young German was following a parallel path. Friedrich Engels, born in 1820, scion of a family of Westphalian industrialists, found himself involved in the ferment of young Hegelianism in Berlin in 1841–2. From the end of 1842 he was employed in the family's cotton mill in Manchester. Here he came into first-hand contact with the new world of industrialization and with new kinds of social antagonisms and new kinds of popular movements such as Chartism, trade unionism and the co-operative movement. Engels brought a very different popular experience to bear on Marx's political thinking in the mid-1840s.

Two independent works by Engels at this time were to play a crucial role in the reorientation of Marx's political thinking. The first, drafted in the autumn of 1843, was his 'Outlines of a Critique of Political Economy'. Here Engels deftly outlined arguments which were to remain central to Marx's political thinking. First was the stress on crisis. Political economy celebrated the law of supply and demand without noticing that far from generating equilibrium, it produced regular and deepening crises of the whole economic order, crises for which political economy had no adequate explanation. Following on from this emphasis on the destabilizing effects of periodic trade crises was a second and related argument. Large capital and large landed estates were continually swallowing up small capital and small estates. This was accelerated in periods of depression so that the whole social order was increasing polarized around extremes of wealth and poverty. The long-term outcome, Engels proposed, was economic collapse and social revolution:

> [A]s long as you continue to produce in the present unconscious, thoughtless manner, at the mercy of chance – for just so long trade crises will remain; and each successive crisis is bound to become more universal and therefore worse than the preceding one; is bound to impoverish a larger body of small capitalists, and to augment in increasing proportion the numbers of the class who live by labour alone, thus considerably enlarging the mass of labour to be employed (the major problem of our economists) and finally causing a social revolution such as has never been dreamt of in the philosophy of the economists. (MECW3: 418ff.)

Engels' essay was read closely by Marx and he published it in the *Deutsch-Französische Jahrbücher* in the following year. In the Preface to *A Contribution to the Critique of Political Economy* in 1859 Marx recalled its importance to his own intellectual development, describing it as a 'brilliant essay on the critique of economic categories'.

At the same time as beginning a critique of political economy, Engels was collecting detailed evidence of working-class conditions, especially in the North of England, cutting edge of the new industrial technologies. This material was pulled together in *The Condition of the Working Class in England*, published in German in 1845. It provided a concrete and thoroughly documented account of the English working class – of wages, working conditions, diet, housing and so on. It also provided an example of how to utilize evidence contained in parliamentary commissions and reports of factory inspectors, something Marx was to do in *Capital* to great effect. There was also a political message for Marx in *The Condition of the Working Class in England*. Engels charted how industrial concentration was creating a new mass working class, through whose organizations, such as trade unions, local economic struggles were becoming national political struggles. New forms of industrial development taking place in Britain were thus creating a new kind of political agent – the proletariat – and a new kind of dynamic between the economic and the political, between the local and the national, between civil society and the state. It was economic and social organization which, thus, provided the key to political issues. Now the proletariat could be identified not merely as the abstract negation of the established reality but as a concrete social force for revolutionary change. Engels pointed the way to a new kind of radical political practice.

Marx came independently to political economy through his own critical engagement with German idealism in the early 1840s. He could hardly avoid it since Adam Smith's *Wealth of Nations* – and particularly his notions of civil society and of the 'unseen hand' of progress – was a central influence on the young Hegel.[2] But Engels' critical and empirical studies reinforced Marx's own critical engagement with political economy. The so-called *Economic and Philosophic Manuscripts of 1844* were initially notes and drafts for his own clarification. Before long they became working drafts for a book to be called *A Critique of Politics and of Political Economy*. By February 1845 Marx had signed a contract with a Darmstadt publisher. What has survived is only part of this uncompleted work, but it indicates how far advanced Marx's critique of capitalism already was by the close of 1844. The manuscript has substantial sections on wages, on capital and how it accrues profit, and on rent. It is based on a close reading of Adam Smith's *The Wealth of Nations* and David Ricardo's *On the Principles of Political Economy and Taxation*, the two great founding texts of nineteenth-century political economy. Thinking within the framework of political economy and utilizing its concepts Marx is able to develop a ringing indictment of contemporary societies:

> We have started out from the premises of political economy. We have accepted its language and its laws. We presupposed private property; the separation of labour, capital, and land, and likewise of wages, profit, and capital; the division of labour; competition; the conception of exchange value, etc. From political economy itself, using its own words, we have shown that the worker sinks to the level of a commodity, and moreover the most wretched commodity of all; that the misery of the worker is in inverse proportion to the power and volume of his production; that the necessary consequence of competition is the accumulation of capital in a few hands and hence the restoration of monopoly in a more terrible form; and that, finally, the distinction between capitalist and landlord, between agricultural

> worker and industrial worker, disappears and the whole of society must split into the two classes of *property owners* and propertyless *workers*. (1975a: 322)

But Marx goes further than this. Probing the presuppositions and the silences of political economy he ruthlessly exposes its limitations. Assuming the fact of private property, of the separation between labour and capital, political economy never asks how these came to exist. Its own abstractions and generalizations are turned into timeless laws:

> We must avoid repeating the mistake of the political economist, who bases his explanations on some imaginary primordial condition. Such a primordial condition explains nothing. It simply pushes the question into the grey and nebulous distance. It assumes as facts and events what it is supposed to deduce – namely, the necessary relationships between two things, between, for example, the division of labour and exchange. Similarly, theology explains the origin of evil by the fall of Man – i.e., it assumes as a fact in the form of history what it should explain. (1975a: 323)

The lever which Marx uses to loosen political economy's apparent fixity is an '*actual* economic fact' – the condition of the working class. How is it, Marx asks, that the worker becomes poorer the more wealth he produces? 'The *devaluation* of the human world grows in direct proportion to the *increase in value* of the world of things'. And political economy itself devalues the human, considering the worker solely as a source of labour. Thus for the political economist, 'the proletarian, the same as any horse, must get as much as will enable him to work': 'It does not consider him when he is not working, as a human being; but leaves such consideration to criminal law, to doctors, to religion, to the statistical tables, to politics and to the poor-house overseer'. In Ricardo's *Principles*, Marx says, 'men are nothing, the product everything': 'Nations are merely workshops for production and man is a machine for consuming and producing. Human life is a piece of capital. Economic laws rule the world blindly' (1975a: 306). Here we already have in succinct form some of the central arguments that Marx was to pursue for the rest of his life.

THE GERMAN IDEOLOGY

These different critical engagements – with German philosophy, French political theory and practice, British political economy – began to fuse into a powerful synthesis. In September 1844 Marx and Engels had spent several weeks together in intense discussion. *The Holy Family*, a rapidly drafted polemic against some of the young Hegelians, was their first joint production. Between the autumn of 1845 and the summer of 1846 they spent more time working together, hammering out their differences with their German contemporaries and elaborating alternative perspectives. The massive unfinished manuscript of *The German Ideology* was the result, though it remained unpublished in their lifetime.

The first part – 'Feuerbach. Opposition of the Materialist and Idealist Outlooks' – is the most important. Here Marx and Engels distinguish their materialist approach from that of their philosophical contemporaries in Germany. 'The first premise of all human history is, of course, the existence of living human individuals', they argue:

> In direct contrast to German philosophy which descends from heaven to earth, here we ascend from earth to heaven. That is to say, we do not set out from what men say, imagine, conceive, nor from men as narrated, thought of, imagined, conceived, in order to arrive at men in the flesh. We set out from real, active men . . . (MECW5: 35)

Any understanding of the past and the present has to focus not on the ideas that people have of themselves but on their active and practical existence in a material world – and primarily on how they extracted a subsistence from their environment. Marx and Engels stress how this material practice is also social – it is a way of life – and thus shapes the character of social relations:

> This mode of production must not be considered simply as being the production of the physical existence of the individuals. Rather it is a definite form of activity of these individuals, a definite form of expressing their life, a definite mode of life on their part. As individuals express their life, so they are. What they are, therefore, coincides with their production, both with what they produce and with

> how they produce. The nature of individuals thus depends on the material conditions determining their production. (MECW5: 32)

What Marx and Engels are already describing as 'the materialist conception of history' is focused on 'the real process of production, starting out from the material production of life itself'. It is this material practice, and the forms of social intercourse connected with it, they argue, which constitutes the basis of all history.

In *The German Ideology* this radical materialism tends to reduce ideology and consciousness to merely passive reflections of the real: 'morality, religion, metaphysics, all the rest of ideology and their corresponding forms of consciousness' are described as 'ideological reflexes and echoes', 'phantoms formed in the human brain', 'sublimates of their material life-process'. As such they are secondary phenomena, outside of a history whose dynamic is now rooted not in human ideas and intentions but in the division of labour – a concept which Marx derives from his close reading of Adam Smith's *Wealth of Nations*. The division of labour is a matter of the technical organization of production to increase productivity and it is always linked to the market. But the division of labour and the market are also forms of social intercourse. It includes the division between town and country and between intellectual and manual labour, for instance. So here we have the crux of Marx's historical theory – exchange and the division of labour and the productive forces interact to generate changes in social relations:

> The division of labour inside a nation leads at first to the separation of industrial and commercial from agricultural labour, and hence to the separation of town and country and to the conflict of their interests. Its further development leads to the separation of commercial from industrial labour. At the same time through the division of labour inside these various branches there develop various divisions among the individuals co-operating in definite kinds of labour. The relative position of these individual groups is determined by the methods employed in agriculture, industry and commerce (patriarchalism, slavery, estates, classes). (MECW5: 32)

So different stages in the development of the division of labour corresponds to different forms of ownership – tribal ownership, communal and state ownership, or feudal ownership, for instance. In the several sections of Part 1 there is some discussion of communism as the inevitable outcome of historical development. In line with the radical materialism of the whole work, this is not envisaged in terms of 'an ideal to which reality will have to adjust itself': 'We call communism the real movement which abolishes the present state of things' (MECW5: 48).

Marx and Engels insist that their historical outline is no more than a set of provisional guidelines. Note the repetition of 'definite' here, stressing the specificity of focus. This is not a philosophical schema but a programme for further empirical investigation:

> The fact is, therefore, that definite individuals who are productively active in a definite way enter into these definite social and political relations. Empirical observation must in each separate instance bring out empirically, and without any mystification and speculation, the connection of the social and political structure with production. The social structure and the State are continually evolving out of the life-process of definite individuals, but of individuals, not as they may appear in their own or other people's imagination, but as they really are; i.e. as they operate, produce materially, and hence as they work under definite material limits, presuppositions and conditions independent of their will. (MECW5: 35)

The German Ideology advances an empirical science of the human world, not a philosophical theory: 'when we conceive things thus, as they really are and happened, every profound philosophical problem is resolved . . . quite simply into an empirical fact.' So philosophy has to be left behind and attention paid instead, 'like an ordinary man to the study of actuality . . .'. Or, in a blunter formulation: 'Philosophy and the study of the actual world have the same relation to one another as onanism and sexual love' (MECW5: 232–8).

Much of the rest of the manuscript of the *German Ideology* is a long and often tedious point-by-point criticism of specific contemporary writers in Germany and in modern editions of *The German Ideology* this is often omitted altogether. However the lengthy first section is one of the most cited of the works of Marx and Engels.

THE COMMUNIST MANIFESTO: THE DYNAMICS OF HISTORY

Written with unusual speed by Marx in a few weeks in January 1848, on the basis of extended discussions with Engels and some working drafts he provided, the *Communist Manifesto* was a short but eloquent statement of many of these critical engagements with German, French and British political thinking over the previous five or six years. Commissioned by the Communist League, an organization of political refugees mostly in London, it was intended to provide a rallying cry for the disorganized ranks of European socialists. Appearing initially in German, there were plans for English, French, Italian, Flemish and Danish editions too.

The *Communist Manifesto* was a powerful work of political rhetoric. It deployed the dramatic vocabulary and radical utopianism of the French Revolution with its stress on popular action and its hope for a new political order built on the smouldering ruins of the old. It was aimed at a broad readership. From its opening line to its last, it was packed with vivid images and memorable slogans and some of its direct and powerful formulations have entered the common language: 'A spectre is haunting Europe – the spectre of communism'; 'The proletarians have nothing to lose but their chains. They have a world to win'. In its opening section the *Communist Manifesto* provides a brilliant sketch of the history of the present – of the rise of the bourgeoisie, its unprecedented economic and social transformation of the world, its political triumphs, but also the social antagonisms between the propertyless and the propertied, between labour and capital, which it generated, leading to revolution and its own self-destruction:

> The history of all hitherto existing society is the history of class struggles. Freeman and slave, patrician and plebeian, lord and serf, guild-master and journeyman, in a word, oppressor and oppressed, stood in constant opposition to one another, carried on an uninterrupted, now hidden, now open fight, a fight that each time ended, either in a revolutionary reconstitution of society at large, or in the common ruin of the contending classes. (2002: 219)

The dynamic of history is the struggle of contending groups. As Marx acknowledges, in earlier periods of history societies were characterized by 'a complicated arrangement of society into various orders, a manifold gradation of social rank'. Thus in the European Middle Ages there were feudal lords, vassals, guild-masters, journeymen, apprentices, serfs and within each of these classes there were further hierarchies. Such complexity stems from a social order in which relations are structured by all kinds of traditions and customs. What is distinctive about contemporary history is the increasing simplification of a social order in which exchange predominates: 'Society as a whole is more and more splitting up into two great hostile camps, into two great classes directly facing each other – Bourgeoisie and Proletariat' (2002: 220).

What drives this revolutionary process? The engine is the market and a new kind of bourgeoisie lifted on a rising tide of international trade:

> The discovery of America, the rounding of the Cape, opened up fresh ground for the rising bourgeoisie. The East-Indian and Chinese markets, the colonisation of America, trade with the colonies, the increase in the means of exchange and in commodities generally, gave to commerce, to navigation, to industry, an impulse never before known, and thereby, to the revolutionary element in the tottering feudal society, a rapid development. (2002: 220)

Trade generated demand which in turn generated new forms of production. The craftsman gives way to larger workshops – manufacturing – in which the division of labour increases output. This in turn gives way to steam-powered machinery and the factory. And carried upwards on this long wave of increasing production and trade was a bourgeoisie accumulating more and more capital. 'We see, therefore, how the modern bourgeoisie is itself the product of a long course of development, of a series of revolutions in the modes of production and of exchange.'

There is no explicit reference to 'so-called primitive accumulation' which, as we will see in Chapter 4, played so decisive a role in *Capital*. Nor is there any discussion of slavery, though colonialism is a central part of the narrative of the expansion of trade and bourgeois power across the globe. There is some discussion of the increasing productive capacities achieved via division of labour and machinery. But it is striking how much of Marx's narrative here is based on the dynamic effects of international trade and the emergence of 'the world market'.

> This market has given an immense development to commerce, to navigation, to communication by land. This development has, in its turn, reacted on the extension of industry; and in proportion as industry, commerce, navigation, railways extended, in the same proportion the bourgeoisie developed, increased its capital, and pushed into the background every class handed down from the Middle Ages. (2002: 221)

Increasing economic power was reflected in growing political power, according to Marx. 'Each step in the development of the bourgeoisie was accompanied by a corresponding political advance of that class'. Oppressed by the feudal nobility, they had carved out a limited space of freedom, initially in medieval towns and later as a counterweight to either absolutist monarchies or the landed classes of early modern Europe. And now 'the bourgeoisie has at last, since the establishment of Modern Industry and of the world market, conquered for itself, in the modern representative State, exclusive political sway. The executive of the modern state is but a committee for managing the common affairs of the whole bourgeoisie' (2002: 221).

The centrepiece of this first section of the *Manifesto* is an exhilarating narrative of the bourgeoisie's rise to power and its prodigious impact on the whole world, penetrating to the innermost relations among people:

> The bourgeoisie, wherever it has got the upper hand, has put an end to all feudal, patriarchal, idyllic relations. It has pitilessly torn asunder the motley feudal ties that bound man to his 'natural superiors', and has left remaining no other nexus between man and man than naked self-interest, than callous 'cash payment'. It has drowned the most heavenly ecstasies of religious fervour, of chivalrous enthusiasm, of philistine sentimentalism, in the icy water of egotistical calculation. It has resolved personal worth into exchange value, and in place of the numberless indefeasible chartered freedoms, has set up that single, unconscionable freedom – Free Trade. In one word, for exploitation, veiled by religious and political illusions, it has substituted naked, shameless, direct, brutal exploitation . . . Constant revolutionising of production,

> uninterrupted disturbance of all social conditions, everlasting uncertainty and agitation distinguish the bourgeois epoch from all earlier ones. All fixed, fast-frozen relations, with their train of ancient and venerable prejudices and opinions, are swept away, all new-formed ones become antiquated before they can ossify. All that is solid melts into air, all that is holy is profaned, and man is at last compelled to face with sober senses his real conditions of life, and his relations with his kind. (2002: 222–3)

From one perspective this is a positive account of the colossal energies unleashed by the new bourgeoisie. It reads like a celebration of a modernity which overshadows all previous periods of history and which, Marx says, 'has been the first to show what man's activity can bring about'. 'It has accomplished wonders far surpassing Egyptian pyramids, Roman aqueducts, and Gothic cathedrals; it has conducted expeditions that put in the shade all former Exoduses of nations and crusades'. And he goes on to itemize the feats of modern science and technology which had subjected the forces of nature to human power: 'what earlier century had even a presentiment that such productive forces slumbered in the lap of social labour?' (2002: 225).

Marx clearly relishes this radical sweeping away of every established idea and institution, every tradition, every custom, every kind of local or national prejudice. At the same time for large numbers of people the consequences are disastrous. The narrative of this first section of the *Communist Manifesto* is riven with the antagonisms of contending forces, by huge destructiveness, by crises and breakdowns, by revolutionary transformations or – and this is particularly important to remember – 'the common ruin of the contending classes'. The dynamic role of the bourgeoisie in sweeping away all that stands in its way is not then some progressive unfolding in a single line of development; but, it is a revolutionary process – and one which creates for the first time in human history the opportunity for human beings to live free from oppression and poverty. Industrial capitalism is not only the antithesis of communism; it is also its essential precondition.

THE COMMUNIST MANIFESTO: A POLITICAL PROGRAMME

Part II of the *Communist Manifesto* turns to immediate political problems and a straightforward question: what then must we do?

What practical measures for change does the *Communist Manifesto* propose? Political power comes first. The first step is to win the battle of democracy. This power will then be used to appropriate, step by step, all capital from the bourgeoisie and to centralize all instruments of production in the hands of the state. Precise measures required to achieve this end will, of course, vary from country to country but, Marx and Engels suggested, some will be 'pretty generally applicable' 'in most advanced countries'. They listed ten. I quote them verbatim here:

1. Abolition of property in land and application of all rents of land to public purposes.
2. A heavy progressive or graduated income tax.
3. Abolition of all rights of inheritance.
4. Confiscation of the property of all emigrants and rebels.
5. Centralisation of credit in the hands of the state, by means of a national bank with State capital and an exclusive monopoly.
6. Centralisation of the means of communication and transport in the hands of the State.
7. Extension of factories and instruments of production owned by the State; the bringing into cultivation of waste-lands, and the improvement of the soil generally in accordance with a common plan.
8. Equal liability of all to work. Establishment of industrial armies, especially for agriculture.
9. Combination of agriculture with manufacturing industries; gradual abolition of all the distinction between town and country by a more equable distribution of the populace over the country.
10. Free education for all children in public schools. Abolition of children's factory labour in its present form. Combination of education with industrial production, &c, &c. (2002: 243–4)

How is this programme to be implemented? The initial stages of the revolution can only be achieved by what they call 'despotic inroads on the rights of property, and on the conditions of bourgeois production'. The concept of 'the dictatorship of the proletariat' is already more or less explicit here. 'The dictatorship of the proletariat' was necessary to organize the defeat of opposing forces in what was more or less a situation of civil war. Vigorous measures for the appropriation of private property were likely to meet strong opposition. As Marx commented after his experience of the 1848 revolution: 'Every provisional political set-up following a revolution requires a dictatorship, and an energetic dictatorship at that' (MECW7: 431). It is also worth remembering that in 1848 there was no unified German state, merely a collection of weak and fragmented local states loosely federated in a customs union and dominated by Prussia and the Hapsburg regime in Vienna. The political landscape of much of central, southern and eastern Europe was dominated by ramshackle semi-feudal multi-national empires – the Austro-Hungarian Empire, the Ottoman Empire and Russia. The despotic revolutionary regime proposed by the *Manifesto*, with its stress on centralization, was thus strategic for building a more coherent nation-state.

This revolutionary 'dictatorship of the proletariat' was not an ideal form of government. It was merely a short-term strategy. According to the *Manifesto*, as these measures to centralize and collectivize private property for the good of all took effect, class distinctions would disappear. Production would be concentrated in the hands of 'a vast association of the whole nation'. Politics and the state would fade away. 'Political power, properly so called, is merely the organised power of one class for oppressing another.' In its challenge to the bourgeoisie, working people are forced to organize themselves into a ruling class. But once it has swept away the old economic, social and political order which sustained class antagonism, this socialist ruling class will also cease to exist: 'In place of the old bourgeois society, with its classes and class antagonisms, we shall have an association, in which the free development of each is the condition for the free development of all' (2002: 244).

The Communist Manifesto sets out the kind of long-term strategies required to transform a capitalist society, based upon private property and the exploitation of the labouring majority, into a communist society where poverty, oppression and conflict are things of the past. But what about immediate political tactics in a pre-revolutionary situation? What do revolutionaries do in the everyday and generally unrevolutionary political situations they find themselves in? The answer the *Manifesto* offers is unremitting opposition to the powers-that-be. 'Communists everywhere support every revolutionary movement against the existing social and political order of things.' But here Marx and Engels carefully distinguish Communist tactics and strategies from other contemporary versions of 'socialism'. Part III of the *Communist Manifesto* is a critical, sometimes ungenerous, survey of various forms of utopian socialism circulating in western Europe in the 1840s. While, in their different ways they voice decent and honourable ideals, Marx is disparaging of the naivety of these pacific, utopian and non-political socialisms. Too often they think that their blueprints for a new economic, social and political order can be introduced peacefully into the world from above and without much political disturbance. They disdain organization or political strategy, much less revolutionary rigour.

Utopian socialists are sharply criticized for their unworldliness. But those rigorous apostles of revolution who followed Babeuf and Blanqui are lambasted for their dangerous and ineffective conspiracies. Marx and Engels shared a deep hostility to insurrectionary adventures which failed to take any measure of the real situation. As the latter had put it in a preliminary draft of the *Manifesto* a few months earlier:

> We are convinced not only of the uselessness but even of the harmfulness of all conspiracies. We are also aware that revolutions are not made deliberately and arbitrarily but that everywhere and at all times they are the necessary consequence of circumstances which are not in any way whatever dependent either on the will or on the leadership of individual parties or of whole classes.[3]

But, however critical Marx and Engels were of other versions of socialism and other forms of radical political action in the 1840s, this did not preclude co-operation in a broad democratic alliance. Everywhere Communists must fight for the immediate and short-term interests of the working class and they must ally with other parties working to the same ends. At the same time they must be aware of longer-term divergences with these political allies.

This was particularly the case in Germany. From the historical narrative of the first part of the *Manifesto*, it seemed to follow that a socialist revolution in 1848 was feasible only in the most advanced capitalist society – England. However, in section 4 of the *Manifesto* it was not England but Germany which featured as the most promising political arena for the Communists. Of course Marx and Engels were German, the Communist League which had commissioned it was mostly made up of German exiles and the *Manifesto* was written in German. But Marx justified this unexpected focus by pointing to Germany's incipient bourgeois revolution which would create the conditions for popular revolution:

> The Communists turn their attention chiefly to Germany, because that country is on the eve of a bourgeois revolution that is bound to be carried out under more advanced conditions of European civilization, and with a much more developed proletariat, than that of England was in the seventeenth, and of France in the eighteenth century, and because the bourgeois revolution in Germany will be but the prelude to an immediately following proletarian revolution. (2002: 258)

This political scenario involved complex political strategies and shifting coalitions. Communists were necessarily brought into alliance with the bourgeoisie, for instance, wherever it was fighting against the absolutist monarchy and the feudal landowners. But Communists, in the words of the *Manifesto*, 'never cease, for a single instant, to instill into the working class the clearest possible recognition of the hostile antagonism between bourgeoisie and proletariat'. Once the bourgeoisie is in the ascendant, Marx says, alliance turns to opposition. Its own weapons are turned against it. 'The fight against the bourgeoisie itself may immediately begin' (2002: 258).

Whatever the specificity of local political conditions, the *Communist Manifesto* advocated the creation of a powerful democratic movement through 'the union and agreement of the democratic parties of all countries'. Note that Marx and Engels were explicit that there is no formal and distinct 'Communist Party' in 1848. 'The Communists do not form a separate party opposed to other working-class parties.' And they added for good measure: 'They do not set up any sectarian principles of their own, by which to shape and mould the proletarian movement.' *The Communist Manifesto* did not, therefore, include all of the key priorities that Marx and Engels had discussed in their pre-1848 writings. There was, for instance, nothing much in the *Manifesto* on abolition of the division of labour, whose crippling effects had been stressed in *The German Ideology*. It is important also to appreciate the immediate historical connotations of the name 'Communist' in 1848.

As Engels' preface to the English edition of the Manifesto in 1888 said: 'when it was written, we could not have called it a *socialist* manifesto'. 'Socialist' at that time designated such utopian sects as the Owenites in England and the Fourierists in France, both in terminal decline by the late 1840s. 'Socialist' was also a name for what Engels termed 'the most multifarious social quacks who, by all manner of tinkering, professed to redress, without any danger to capital and profit, all sorts of social grievances'. 'Communist' on the other hand, was a term for those who saw the need for revolutionary social and political transformation, 'Thus, in 1847, socialism was a middle-class movement, communism a working-class movement. Socialism was, on the Continent at least, "respectable"; communism was the very opposite' (2002: 202).

1848: REVOLUTION AND COUNTER-REVOLUTION

Rarely has a political programme been brought so quickly to the test. Within weeks of the *Manifesto*'s publication, revolutions swept across Europe toppling regimes in Paris, Berlin, Vienna and elsewhere. After some difficulties with the Brussels police and then a few weeks in revolutionary Paris, Marx was back in Cologne by April and embroiled in revolutionary politics. The Communist League itself was too few in numbers to function as a political party. Marx and Engels therefore took the line that League members could best serve the revolution by active participation in the various workers' associations and democratic societies which were being formed throughout Germany. Marx and Engels themselves joined the Cologne Democratic Society. They also set up a daily newspaper: the *Neue Rheinische Zeitung*: *Organ der Democratie*, with Marx as its editor-in-chief. Its first number appeared on 1 June 1848.

The problem facing the German Communists in 1848 was how to balance short-term tactics with longer-term goals. Marx opposed insurrectionary adventures and pointless confrontations with authority and he was committed to public agitation. However, in a Germany which in 1848 remained at the earliest stages of development both in economic and political terms, there was not much in the way of an industrial working class and thus any moves towards socialist revolution were surely premature. For Marx, political will must always be subordinated to what was practically achievable in any concrete political, social and economic situation. And yet abstention from the political realities of a Germany in revolution was hardly an option either and would result in political isolation. Marx's strategy, therefore, influenced by the practical lessons he drew from the French Revolution, involved tactical alliances with other social groups, first the bourgeoisie and second, the peasantry.

'Demands of the Communist Party in Germany', exemplify this commitment to some kind of broad democratic alliance. Drafted by Marx and Engels in Paris in March 1848, and approved as the official programme of the Communist League, it was printed and reprinted as a leaflet and published in several newspapers throughout Germany's revolutionary year. It was carefully calibrated to appeal to a broad range of popular demands. It called for the creation of a united republican Germany, for universal male suffrage, for the arming of the people, for the payment of representatives so that working men could afford to be elected to parliament. It called for the creation of a state bank and the nationalization of the means of transport, railways, canals, steamships, roads, the posts and of royal and feudal estates (1973a: 109–10).

There was a measure of 'to each according to his needs' when the imposition of a single wage for all civil servants had an exemption for those with a family to support and who, therefore, had greater needs. Struggling craftsmen and domestic workers were appealed to via the creation of 'national workshops': 'The state is to guarantee all workers their existence and care for those unable to work' (1973a: 110). Marx himself was somewhat sceptical about this half-hearted gesture towards communism. The *droit au travail*, the right to work, included in the first draft of the constitution that followed the February revolution in France, was, he said, 'a preliminary, clumsy formula, summarizing the revolutionary claims of the proletariat'. But the reality that followed was the *droit a l'assistance*, the right to poor relief, and this was merely another way in which paupers were fed. Marx had already identified the decisive role of a reserve army of labour in the reproduction of capitalist relations of production; in other words, full employment was impossible in an economy in which labour-power was a commodity sold in the market:

> The right to work is, in the bourgeois sense, nonsense, a wretched, pious wish. But behind the right to work stands power over capital; behind power over capital, the appropriation of the means of production, their subjection to the associated working class,

> that is, the abolition of wage labor, capital and their mutual relationship. (1973b: 69–70)

So Marx supported 'the right to work' precisely because it was an unrealistic demand, one that pointed beyond the capitalist present to a different kind of future in which there would be no capital, no wage labour, no unemployment.

Other demands of the Communists in Germany, appealing to a wide social spectrum, included the provision of free legal services, the creation of free and universal education, the disestablishment of the Church. Several measures, including the abolition of all feudal obligations, dues, corvées, tithes and so on, were designed to reduce the burden of taxation on peasants and small tenant farmers. And the leaflet ended with an appeal to 'the German proletariat, the petty bourgeoisie and the small peasants' to work together to support the 17 points of this programme:

> Through their realization alone can the millions of German people, who have up till now been exploited by a small handful, and whom some will attempt to maintain in renewed oppression, get their rights, and the power that they are due as the producers of all wealth. (1973a: 110–11)

For Marx political co-operation would always be tactical and in the long run, he believed, doomed to failure. His strategy therefore was to guide the masses through temporary alliances and inevitable defeats towards ultimate political enlightenment, especially about the limits of 'bourgeois-democracy'. The German proletariat had to *experience* a democratic revolution in order to understand the social limitations of formal political equality. Writing in the *Neue Rheinische Zeitung* at the end of 1848, Marx said: 'The chief result of the revolutionary movement of 1848 is not what the peoples won, but what they lost – the *loss of their illusions*.' The brutal repression of the June Days in Paris and the violent suppression of the popular uprising in Vienna in October and November 1848, thoroughly documented in the pages of the *Neue Rheinische Zeitung*, were, he went on, 'gigantic milestones on the path to the disenchantment and disintoxication of the minds of the European peoples' (MECW 8: 197).

For nearly a year, under the editorial command of Marx, the *Neue Rheinische Zeitung* was a powerful voice of the democratic left in Germany, despite its modest readership of around 6,000. Its uncompromising support for the defeated Paris insurrection in June 1848 had alienated many of its liberal middle-class readers and its existence was increasingly uncertain. Its prosecution was urged by members of the Frankfurt parliament and publication was suspended briefly in the autumn of 1848. After the Prussian coup in November 1848 the *Neue Rheinische Zeitung* called for non-payment of taxes and the resistance of force by force. Marx was brought before the courts twice on charges of incitement to armed resistance to the government. Both times he was acquitted. Finally in May 1849 the government closed the paper down and Marx was expelled from Prussia. The final issue of the *Neue Rheinische Zeitung* was printed in red ink and its farewell address concluded: 'Their last word, always and everywhere will be: *the emancipation of the working class*' (1973a: 264).

Back in Paris, a political refugee again, Marx was identified by the French government as a dangerous subversive. He was offered permission to live in France only if he remained far from Paris in southern Brittany. Instead, planning a revived expatriate newspaper, he chose exile and in the summer of 1849 he became one of the thousands of European political refugees who escaped across the channel to London. Here Marx resumed his work as a political journalist. The *Neue Rheinische Zeitung, Politisch-Okonomische Revue* was launched as a monthly journal. It struggled with limited financial backing and insufficient subscribers. After the fourth edition in April 1850 there was a long gap, before a final joint issue, numbers 5 and 6, was published in November 1850. At the same time, Marx's political hopes began to fade. In March, 1850, the Central Committee of the Communist League, most of whom had now regrouped in London, issued a circular drawn up by Marx and Engels. Confident that a new revolution was imminent in France and Germany, it called on revolutionary workers to ally with petty-bourgeois democrats but to be prepared to take a more radical direction. Initially there was some success. However, during the summer of 1850 it was becoming obvious to Marx that the revolutionary wave was receding. There would be no renewal of the revolutionary movement until another major economic crisis occurred. Any attempt to force a revolution, to induce an uprising, was doomed to defeat. Divisions within the Central Committee culminated in September 1850 in a split. The minority who opposed a more realistic assessment of the political possibilities of the present situation were told by Marx that they paid too much attention to their own desires for revolution. 'We tell the workers: If you want to change conditions and make yourselves capable of government, you will have to undergo fifteen, twenty, or even fifty years of civil war' (1973a: 341). Marx was to withdraw, half unwillingly, from much in the way of active politics for the next 15 years.

CHAPTER 3

MATERIALIST HISTORIES

> History *does* nothing, *it 'possesses* no *immense wealth', it 'wages* no *battles'. It is* man, *real, living man who does all that, who possesses and fights; 'history' is not, as it were, a person apart, using man as a means to achieve* its own *aims; history is* nothing but *the activity of man pursuing his aims.*
>
> *(MECW4: 92–3)*

> *Whilst in ordinary life every shopkeeper is very well able to distinguish between what someone professes to be and what he really is, our historiography has not yet won even this trivial insight. It takes every epoch at its word and believes that everything it says and imagines about itself is true.*
>
> *(MECW5: 62)*

From the end of 1850, with the closure of his short-lived journal and the disintegration of the Communist League, Marx entered a period of relative political isolation. Engels returned to Manchester to resume work for Ermen & Engels. Marx never entirely insulated himself from the squabbles of the London exiles and he kept in touch with a number of the old veterans of 1848. He also maintained some links with political radicals in England, notably the leading Chartist Ernest Jones.

However, despite his conviction that economic crises were inevitable, with huge potential for the revival of revolutionary politics, Marx saw little future for the political exiles and groupuscules that had survived from 1848. Rapid economic development was making their revolutionary rhetoric increasingly irrelevant to a rapidly changing economic and social world. For instance, in a newspaper article on the monetary crisis in Europe in October 1856, Marx pointed to the importance of the new financial institutions of ascendent capitalism – 'the instruments of a revolution in property greater than any contemplated by the revolutionists of 1848'. In the face of this revolution from above, the old conspiratorial organizations of the left had little to offer. 'They know nothing of the economical life of people, they know nothing of the real conditions of historical movement, and when the new revolution shall break out they will have a better right than Pilate to wash their hands and protest that they are innocent of bloodshed' (MECW15: 113–14). After 1852 Marx was not associated with *any* political organization, public or secret. He was, he assured one of his old revolutionary comrades in 1860, 'firmly convinced that my theoretical studies were of greater use to the working class than my meddling with associations which had now had their day on the Continent' (MECW41: 80). Finding it increasingly impossible to exert any influence on Germany from abroad, Marx was glad, as Engels put it, 'to find once more some quiet time for research work'.

This research work never took Marx very far from the political realities around him. While studying in the British Museum, he was also working as a political journalist, building up a detailed knowledge of British and international politics, institutions and movements during the 1850s. This influenced his own political thinking and fed into his drafting and redrafting of *Grundrisse* and *Capital.* In nearly 500 articles for the *New York Daily Tribune*, over 100 for *Neue Oder Zeitung* and around 175 for *Die Presse*, all written between 1852 and 1862, Marx gave some proof of his commitment to 'conscientious investigation', enforced though it was by the need to earn some money. He grumbled frequently about having to spend his days working on these articles. Some were superficial hack work, drafted quickly to meet a deadline while his mind was on other things. Some were fairly straightforward commentary. But some of his journalism required research and gave Marx detailed knowledge of a broad range of contemporary economic and political matters. If, as Marx grumbled, his work for the *New York Tribune* 'necessitated an excessive fragmentation of my studies', it also compelled him 'to become conversant with practical detail which, strictly speaking, lie outside the sphere of political economy'. Journalistic hack work was not then irrelevant to Marx's theoretical labours.[1] It also, incidentally, stimulated Marx to become fluent in English. Already in 1851 Marx was engaged in a formidable programme of reading in the British Museum, much of it in English. But Engels ascribed some recent tensions with leading Chartists such as Harney to the fact that, as he put it, 'Marx speaks little English' (MECW38:380). In the following year his first articles for the *New York Tribune* were drafted in German and translated into English by Engels. But by the beginning of 1853 Marx was writing in English himself.

In this chapter, I will focus on two clusters of work by Marx from these years: first, several discussions of the political landscape of Europe before and after 1848; and second, his critical investigations into political economy, part of his search for a different kind of revolutionary politics.

AFTER 1848: POLITICS AND CLASS

Marx was to ponder the political lessons of 1848 for the rest of his life. In particular, he was forced to rethink his earlier conceptions of the state. The *Communist Manifesto* had emphasized how the economic and social rise of the bourgeoisie was accompanied by a corresponding political ascendency. But this had been posed in simple terms: 'The executive of the modem state is but a committee for managing the common affairs of the whole bourgeoisie' (2002: 221). In other words, the state was an instrument of particular economic and social interests and the accession of the emerging capitalist class to direct political power was both necessary and inevitable.

When the grasp of the bourgeoisie on political power in Germany weakened at the end of 1848, Marx warned in the pages of the *Neue Rheinische Zeitung* that its long-term economic interests would be fatally damaged by the restoration of an old regime of landowners, bureaucrats and army officers with a king at its head. 'Does history provide a single example showing that under a king imposed by the grace of God, the bourgeoisie ever succeeded in attaining a form of government in keeping with its material interests?' The fate of the Stuarts in seventeenth-century Britain and the Bourbons in eighteenth-century France demonstrated the contrary:

> Bourgeois industry must burst the chains of absolutism and feudalism. A revolution against both only demonstrates that

> bourgeois industry has reached a level when it must either secure an appropriate political form or perish. (MECW8: 258f.)

However, after the defeats of the 1848 revolutions, conservative regimes and state formations were once more in the ascendant across Europe. This required some rethinking of the confident assertion of the *Communist Manifesto*, that society was increasingly dividing 'into two great hostile camps, into two great classes directly facing each other – Bourgeoisie and Proletariat'. During the 1848 revolutions and their aftermath social classes failed to organize and act as collective political actors in any very straightforward way. At the same time, the organizations and groupings which were active in the political sphere did not seem to represent directly specific social classes.

Even in Britain the relations between economic, social and political power were a good deal more complex than he had initially assumed. In some of his journalistic writings of the 1850s Marx puzzled over the odd sight of the most advanced industrial economy on the planet being governed by an ancient monarchy and a landed aristocracy. How was it that the great Whig landed families continued to be elected to government in capitalist Britain? 'The British Whig, in the natural history of politics, forms a species which, like all those of the amphibious class, exists very easily, but is difficult to describe'. Marx concluded that though the Whig aristocracy governed it did not exert real power:

> The Whigs are the *aristocratic representatives* of the bourgeoisie, of the industrial and commercial middle class. Under the condition that the Bourgeoisie should abandon to them, to an oligarchy of aristocratic families, the monopoly of government and the exclusive possession of office, they make to the middle class, and assist it in conquering, all those concessions, which in the course of social and political development have shown themselves to have become *unavoidable* and *undelayable*. (MECW11: 328–9)

This alliance of landowners with rising economic and social forces had been the political *modus operandi* of the Whigs since the Glorious Revolution of 1688. They had attached themselves to new banking and financial interests in the City during the eighteenth century, just as in the 1840s they allied themselves with the northern industrialists who led the Anti-Corn Law League. The Great Reform Act of 1832 and the repeal of he Corn Laws in 1846 were bourgeois measures, but under the parliamentary direction of the Whigs who were willing to make short-term sacrifices of their economic interests to preserve their traditional political authority.

In Marx's view, it was the Manchester School that was the legitimate representative of the industrial bourgeoisie in the 1850s: rigorously free market in economic policy, utilitarian in its social philosophy, anti-aristocratic in its political instincts.[2] Compromise with the Whig aristocracy had short-term political advantages for the middle class but, Marx thought, it was an alliance whose days were numbered. The industrial middle class would necessarily assert their dominance:

> They cannot avoid fulfilling their mission, battering to pieces Old England, the England of the Past; and the very moment when they will have conquered exclusive political dominion, when political dominion and economical supremacy will be united in the same hands, when, therefore, the struggle against capital will no longer be distinct from the struggle against the existing Government – from that very moment will date the *social revolution* of England. (MECW11: 334–5)

And yet the moment of unequivocal bourgeois domination of the British state never quite arrived. Marx and Engels continued to reflect on some of the apparent discrepancies between the economic, social and political dimensions of industrial capitalism in Victorian Britain.[3]

THE EIGHTEENTH BRUMAIRE OF LOUIS BONAPARTE

Perhaps the most remarkable challenge to the political projections of the *Communist Manifesto* was the situation of France: how had the February revolution culminated in the autocratic regime of Louis Bonaparte, a character who seemed to represent no significant economic or social interest? Marx drafted several important pieces of historical interpretation of the 1848 revolution in France in which he began to rethink both the social character of the state and the kind of historical narrative outlined in his writings of the 1840s, especially in the *Communist Manifesto*.

The Class Struggles in France first appeared in the form of three substantial articles – 'The Defeat of June 1848', 'June 13, 1849' and 'Consequences of June 13, 1849' – published in the pages of the *Neue Rheinische Zeitung* during 1850.[4] It provided some brilliant analyses of the history of the French state and in particular of how the July Monarchy, installed after the revolution of 1830, represented not the bourgeoisie as a whole but one section of it: the financial aristocracy of bankers, stockmarket barons, railway barons, large landowners and owners of mines. 'The July Monarchy was nothing more than a joint-stock company for the exploitation of France's national wealth, whose dividends were divided among ministers, parliament, 240,000 voters and their adherents' (1973b: 38). Louis Philippe, the king, was merely the director of this company. In a ferocious diatribe, with many resonances today, Marx exposed this regime as one huge financial gambling house riddled by greed and deceit, appropriating the wealth produced by others for the exorbitant indulgences of a narrow elite:

> While the financial aristocracy made the laws, controlled the state administration, exercised authority in all public institutions and controlled public opinion by actual events and through the press, the same prostitution, the same blatant swindling, the same mania for self-enrichment – not from production but by sleight-of-hand with other people's wealth – was to be found in all spheres of society . . . (1973b: 39)

If the French state under the July Monarchy was an instrument of particular economic interests, it was certainly not the interests of the bourgeoisie as a whole. France in the 1830s and 1840s was an altogether more complex economic, social and political formation than that.

Marx's richly documented narrative of the February revolution then tracked the complex social and political forces contending for power in France during 1848 and 1849. It was the story of a series of defeats for the working class, defeats that Marx said were essential for the revolution's ultimate success. What was lost during 1848 and 1849 were obsolete traditions, ideas and illusions. When finally confronted by 'a powerful and united counter-revolution' only then, Marx says, 'did the insurrectionary party mature into a real party of revolution' (1973b: 35). The June days, in which a gigantic popular insurrection in Paris led to five days of bitter fighting and thousands of deaths, revealed in the cold light of day how, despite all the complexities of political parties and ideologies, the struggle was really between 'the two great classes which divide modern society': 'The veil which shrouded the republic was torn asunder'. And so, Marx says, reaffirming the primary antagonism between capital and labour, the republic was forced to reveal itself as a state 'whose avowed purpose is to perpetuate the rule of capital and the slavery of labour' (1973b: 58–9, 61).

The Eighteenth Brumaire of Louis Bonaparte, first published in 1852, took these questions further. In the immediate aftermath of the remarkable coup of December 1851, Marx puzzled over the profound incongruity between the gigantic significance of this event and the apparent insignificance of its hero, Louis Bonaparte:

> The Constitution, the National Assembly, the dynastic parties, the blue and the red republicans, the heroes of Africa, the thunder from the platform, the sheet lightning of the daily press, all the other publications, the political names and the intellectual reputations, the civil law and the penal code, *liberté, egalité, fraternité* and the second Sunday in May, 1852 – all have vanished like a series of optical illusions before the spell of a man whom even his enemies do not claim to be a magician. (1973b: 151)

How could this remarkable event be understood? In his Preface to *The Eighteenth Brumaire's* second edition of 1869, Marx pinpointed two complementary errors, represented by two of the most important and influential contemporary accounts.[5] On the one hand, in his long diatribe *Napoleon le Petit*, the great French novelist Victor Hugo provided a devastating and courageous attack on the new regime. However, there was no historical explanation of how this successful coup d'etat was possible: 'the event itself appears in his work like a bolt from the blue'. By focusing all his furious attention on Louis Bonaparte, he ascribed to him 'a personal power of initiative which would be without precedent in world history'. Hugo succeeded in representing him not as 'Napoleon the little' but in fact as a political colossus. Proudhon, on the other hand, in his *La Révolution sociale demontrée par le coup d'état du 2 décembre 1851*, represents the coup as the inevitable outcome of historical development. Thus, inadvertently, 'his historical construction of the coup d'etat becomes a historical apologia for its hero'. Louis Bonaparte becomes the inevitable expression and instrument of History itself (1973b: 144). In the same way Hegel was supposed to have described Napoleon, when he saw him after his victory at the battle of Jena, as 'world-history on horseback'.

Marx describes his own account of the 1851 coup as a demonstration of 'how the class struggle in France created circumstances and relationships that made it possible for a grotesque mediocrity to play a hero's part' (1973b: 144). In other words, Louis Bonaparte is neither the creator of his own destiny nor the effect of an inevitable historical logic. History is untidier than that. In Marx's account there is some room for contingency and for individuals, groups and organizations to play an active role within the constantly unstable limits of specific situations.[6] In handling the complexities of a precise sequence of events in France in the 1830s and 40s, these works of contemporary history elaborated a very careful and empirically controlled periodization of recent French political history and marked a development beyond the schemas of the 1840s. In his critical studies of Hegel and the French Revolution in 1843 and 1844, as we have seen, Marx talked about the state as the sphere of an abstract and ideal universality. The point was made bluntly in a marginal note to *The German Ideology*: 'all struggles within the State, the struggle between democracy, aristocracy, and monarchy, the struggle for the franchise, etc., etc., are merely the illusory forms in which the real struggles of the different classes are fought out among one another' (MECW5: 46). This was part of *The German Ideology*'s uncompromising emphasis on the 'material' and the 'economic': 'morality, religion, metaphysics, all the rest of ideology and their corresponding forms of consciousness' are described as 'ideological reflexes and echoes', 'phantoms formed in the human brain', 'sublimates of their material life-process'. Empty of significance, they become merely derivative phenomena, outside of history: 'They have no history, no development; but men, developing their material production and their material intercourse, alter, along with this their real existence, their thinking and the products of their thinking' (MECW5: 35–6). Even *The Communist Manifesto*, that most activist of texts, had stressed how the revolutionary role of the bourgeoisie in the overthrow of feudalism and of every trace of the past was fundamentally through the agency of exchange and the penetration of the free market into every sphere of social life. The capture of state power followed somehow as the inevitable consequence.

In *The Eighteenth Brumaire* Marx rejects this kind of unhistorical materialism. The sphere of the political is no longer merely a matter of 'illusory forms' or the effects of struggles for power occurring elsewhere. He explores how constitutions, political alliances, electoral procedures, traditions and ideologies, the whole terrain of political life, had their own material effects and were never merely the shadowy reflection of some prior economic or material reality. Marx accepted that capital and labour did not appear on the political stage 'in person'. Contending political groups 'represented' wider social forces in different ways – and these forces were not limited to 'capitalists' and 'workers'. For instance, the history of the Constituent National Assembly after the June days was the history of the domination and the disintegration of the republican faction of the bourgeoisie. This political grouping was not, Marx says, held together by any great common interests or rooted in specific conditions of production. They were not, in other words, a specific socio-economic grouping. Instead, it was a group constituted by political experiences and political ideologies:

> [I]t was a coterie of republican-minded members of the bourgeoisie, writers, lawyers, officers and officials. Its influence rested on the personal antipathies of the country to Louis Philippe, on memories of the old republic, on the republican faith of a number of enthusiasts, and, above all, on *French nationalism*, for it constantly kept alive hatred of the Vienna treaties and the alliance with England. (1973b: 157)

In the powerful opening paragraphs of *The Eighteenth Brumaire* the past itself is shown to determine the present: 'Hegel says somewhere that all the great events and characters of world history occur, so to speak, twice. He forgot to add: the first time as tragedy, the second time as farce' (1973b: 146–7).[7] If human beings make their own history, they do so always at a specific time and a specific place and thus within a specific set of inherited circumstances:

> The tradition of the dead generations weighs like a nightmare on the minds of the living. And, just when they appear to be

> engaged in the revolutionary transformation of themselves and their material surroundings, in the creation of something which does not exist, precisely in such epochs of revolutionary crisis they timidly conjure up the spirits of the past to help them; they borrow their names, slogans and costumes so as to stage the new world-historical scene in this venerable disguise and borrowed language. Luther put on the mask of the apostle Paul; the Revolution of 1789–1814 draped itself alternately as the Roman republic and the Roman empire; and the revolution of 1848 knew no better than to parody at some points 1789 and at others the revolutionary traditions of 1793–5. (1973b: 146–7)

The French Revolution of 1789–94 draped itself in the costume of Rome in ways which effectively mobilized the passions and the imaginations of men in a struggle which demanded an heroic and selfless commitment – a commitment unlikely to be galvanized by the mundane economic priorities which were the revolution's essential rationale. But once the old feudal structures of France had been demolished, the resurrected images of Rome dissolved and the prosaic realities of bourgeois politics asserted themselves. In the same way, Marx says, the seventeenth-century English revolution had personified itself in 'the language, passions and illusions' of the Old Testament. But puritan martyrs and revolutionaries were eventually replaced by the calculating businessmen of Hanoverian England: 'When the actual goal had been reached, when the bourgeois transformation of English society had been accomplished, Locke drove out Habakkuk' (1973b: 148).

By contrast, in the French Revolution and counterrevolution of 1848–51 the past is not exploited as a resource to transform the present through decisive action. On the contrary, history reasserts its authority over the present and the future. Here there was, Marx says, a 'relapse into the past': an entire social order 'suddenly found itself plunged back into an already dead epoch'. Riddled by internal conflicts, with no faction strong enough to achieve power, France in the aftermath of the revolution of February 1848 'appears to have fallen back behind its starting point'. Seeking a resolution, they looked to the past – and increasingly to that great colossus who, 50 years before, had resolved the insoluble oppositions of the earlier revolution: Napoleon. Eerily, he appeared in the form of his nephew, Louis. Elected president of the new French Republic by a large majority in December 1848, he engineered a coup in December 1851 which finally terminated the revolution:

> As long as the French were engaged in revolution, they could not free themselves of the memory of Napoleon. . . . They have not merely acquired a caricature of the old Napoleon, they have the old Napoleon himself, in the caricature form he had to take in the middle of the nineteenth century. (1973b: 149)

So the nephew not only parodies the uncle; he also, inadvertently, criticizes him by indicating the first Napoleon's own self-parody. This is the occasion for some brilliant satirical writing about the new regime and its own absurd parodies of Napoleonic grandeur.

However, the apotheosis of Louis Bonaparte also raised important questions for Marx about the relations between political actors and economic and social forces in nineteenth-century capitalism. 'Bonapartism' does not fit any simple class model. It is not easily assimilable to the socio-economic antagonisms which Marx posits as the engine of historical change. Nevertheless, there was finally an explanation for this strange reappearance – one rooted in the economic, social and political realities of France. After nearly four years of political turmoil, Bonaparte was increasingly identified by a range of social groups as the best chance for a restoration of order. 'The struggle seems to have reached the compromise that all classes fall on their knees, equally mute and equally impotent, before the rifle-butt' (1973b: 236). Though the Bonapartist state seemed to float free of any social constituency, it was not suspended in mid-air. It did represent one class, the most numerous class in French society and one pretty much ignored by the different political groupings struggling for power in the revolution of 1848: the small-holding peasants.

The Eighteenth Brumaire is a marvellous work of contemporary history – detailed, complex, subtle, a tour de force. Engels referred to it on several occasions as a model of how Marx's general theory could be applied in a precise case-study. It was, he told one correspondent, 'an especially remarkable example'. Answering another correspondent about the causal weight of economic factors in Marx's historical theory he commented: 'the fine example which Marx has given in the *Eighteenth Brumaire* should already, I think, provide you fairly well with information on your questions, just because it is a practical example.' And against a critic who had charged Marx and Engels with underestimating the importance of the political factor in history he directed him to the *Eighteenth Brumaire* which, he says, 'deals almost exclusively with the particular part played by political struggles and events' (1975b: 396, 401–2, 443).

However, Marx did not pursue further investigations into the significance of 1848 in other parts of Europe. Nor did he produce similar kinds of political histories of the present during the 1850s and 1860s, though this was a period of remarkable revolutionary transformation among many of the major capitalist states. The Unification of Germany under Bismarck, the creation of a new unified Italy, the defeat of the slave-owning South at the hands of the industrial North in the United States – all these events of huge international significance failed to draw from Marx any substantial analysis.[8] In the 1850s and 60s Marx was preoccupied with other kinds of questions, not abandoning political analysis of the present but approaching it through a deeper engagement with political economy.

POLITICAL STABILITY AND ECONOMIC CRISIS

In an extended survey of the European political situation in the autumn of 1850, Marx and Engels proposed that a new and unprecedented period of industrial prosperity postponed any question of revolutionary action:

> With this general prosperity, in which the productive forces of bourgeois society develop as luxuriantly as is at all possible within bourgeois relationships, *there can be no talk of a real revolution.* Such a revolution is only possible in the periods when both these factors, the modern productive forces and the bourgeois productive forms, come in collision with each other. (MECW10: 490)

But, they went on to suggest, this collision would not be long delayed: 'If the new cycle of industrial development which began in 1848 takes the same course as that of 1843–7, the crisis will break out in 1852.' As the correspondence of Marx and Engels reveals, they continued to think that some kind of profound economic crisis was imminent throughout the 1850s, with the potential to turn into a revolutionary political situation at any time. 'There seems little doubt about the advent of the crisis, even if the recent bankruptcies were no more than precursors', Marx told Engels in August 1852: 'At all events, whether a revolution is immediately produced – immediately, that is, in 6–8 months – very largely depends on the intensity of the crisis' (MECW39: 162–3, 165).

When a banquet was held in April 1856 to commemorate the fourth anniversary of the Chartist *People's Paper*, Marx was invited to speak as a representative of the revolutionary refugees in London. He gave a brief but blood-curdling speech in his own faltering English. The revolutions of 1848 were, he said, no more than 'small fractures and fissures in the dry crust of European society'. Underneath the apparently solid surface of contemporary bourgeois society there was a volcano ready 'to rend into fragment continents of hard rock': 'On the one hand, there have started into life industrial and scientific forces, which no epoch of the former human history has ever suspected. On the other hand, there exist symptoms of decay, far surpassing the horrors recorded of the latter times of the Roman Empire.' And, he went on, 'everything seems pregnant with its opposite' – labour-saving machinery and overwork, immense wealth and desperate poverty, mastery over nature and human slavery, new scientific knowledge and the deepest ignorance. He concluded with a spine-chilling reference to the *Vehmgericht*, a secret tribunal which exercised great power in medieval Westphalia. If a red cross was marked on a house, everyone knew its inhabitants were doomed. 'All the houses of Europe', Marx said, meaning the ruling families, 'are now marked with the mysterious red cross. History is the judge – its executioner, the proletariat' (1973b: 299–300).

This was not entirely political rabble-rousing over a few drinks among friends, though it was not written for publication. Marx was convinced that economic turbulence was inevitable, with destabilizing political consequences. A major financial crisis would strike by the end of 1857, he was assuring Engels a few months later, looking forward to some political action: 'This time, by the by, the thing has assumed European dimensions such as have never been seen before, and I don't suppose we'll be able to spend much longer here merely as spectators . . . the 'mobilisation' of our persons is at hand' (MECW40: 71). Engels rubbed his hands with glee at the prospect: 'This time there'll be a *dies irae* such as has never been seen before: the whole of Europe's industry in ruins, all markets over-stocked . . . , all the propertied classes in the soup, complete bankruptcy of the bourgeoisie, war and profligacy to the nth degree' (MECW40: 74).

The long-expected financial crisis did arrive, rocking the whole international economy. It stimulated Marx to a burst of writing, drafting the hundreds of pages of notebooks, later assembled as the *Grundrisse*. As he told Lassalle in December 1857: 'The present commercial crisis has impelled me to set to work seriously on my outlines of political economy.' And he wrote to Engels: 'I am working like mad all night and every night collating my economic studies so that I at least get the outlines clear before the *déluge*' (MECW 40: 214). Hopes for a return to Germany and to revolutionary action were again disappointed. By the autumn of 1858 it was clear that the crisis had passed and another boom was underway.

GRUNDRISSE AND THE '1859 PREFACE'

Marx's eager attention to the economic instabilities of the 1850s, combined with his intensive studies of political economy in the British Museum and his political journalism, fed into two important texts at the end of the 1850s: first, the unpublished notebooks that make up the *Grundrisse*; and second, *A Contribution to a Critique of Political Economy*, published in 1859.

The former consists of seven notebooks, entitled by its first editors *Grundrisse der Kritik der politischen Okonomie (Rohentwurf)* – in English: *Foundations of the Critique of Political Economy (Rough Draft)*. Written between the summer of 1857 and the summer of 1858, this is a massive draft; its English translation fills over 800 closely printed pages. Here Marx pulled together his years of study of political economy into a critical analysis of both political economy and contemporary capitalism. There was a brief, unfinished but important introduction in which Marx sketched out some of the methodological foundations for his critique of political economy and provided an outline of his projected study:

> The order obviously has to be (1) the general, abstract determinants which obtain in more or less all forms of society . . . (2) The categories which make up the inner structure of bourgeois society and on which the fundamental classes rest. Capital, wage labour, landed property. Their interrelation. Town and country. The three great social classes. Exchange between them. Circulation.

> Credit system (private). (3) Concentration of bourgeois society in the form of the state. Viewed in relation to itself. The 'unproductive' classes. Taxes. State debt. Public credit. The population. The colonies. Emigration. (4) The international relation of production. International division of labour. International exchange. Export and import. Rate of exchange. (5) The world market and crises. (1973: 108)

Though subsequently modified several times, this remained more or less Marx's master plan for his great work: volumes on capital, wage-labour and rent were to be followed by volumes on the state, international trade and the world market.

The remainder of *Grundrisse* consists of a substantial 'Chapter on Money' (220 pages) followed by a huge 'Chapter on Capital' (640 pages). The whole work was intended as a working draft through which Marx could formulate his key ideas, before reworking the material into publishable forms. So *Grundrisse* was intentionally left incomplete, unstructured, full of compressed formulations, loose ends and undeveloped ideas. As such, it has proved to be a treasure-trove for later commentators and it contains not just central concepts and arguments to be found in *Capital*, but also valuable materials which Marx never got round to developing further.[9]

One section of the *Grundrisse* in particular has attracted considerable interest: a lengthy section (40 or so pages) at the end of Notebook IV and the beginning of Notebook V. It is headed: 'Forms which precede capitalist production. (Concerning the process which precedes the formation of the capital relation or of original accumulation)'. Though the full text of *Grundrisse* was only published in English in 1973, this historical section was published separately in 1964 as *Pre-Capitalist Economic Formations*.[10] It built on work in *The German Ideology*, where Marx and Engels had identified a series of historical stages in the social division of labour corresponding to different forms of property. Marx had studied this question further in the 1850s and was planning a historical study of pre-capitalist modes of production. The *Grundrisse* material was a draft of this work-in-progress, never completed. However, it did feed into discussions in *Capital*, especially the long and important account of original accumulation (or primitive accumulation as it is more commonly translated). This is explored further in the next chapter.

One completed work followed quite quickly from the *Grundrisse*. Published in Germany in 1859, *A Contribution to the Critique of Political Economy* deployed some of the material from the 'Chapter on Money' in the *Grundrisse*. But the book fell flat and, lacking the more important and challenging material on capital, is one of the least read and least discussed of Marx's writings. Its brief preface, however, has had a remarkable influence. It is a widely quoted, even canonical, summary of the working principles of what subsequently became known as the materialist interpretation of history, or historical materialism:

> In the social production of their existence, men inevitably enter into definite relations, which are independent of their will, namely relations of production appropriate to a given stage in the development of their material forces of production. The totality of these relations of production constitutes the economic structure of society, the real foundation, on which arises a legal and political superstructure and to which correspond definite forms of social consciousness. The mode of production of material life conditions the general process of social, political, and intellectual life. It is not the consciousness of men that determines their existence, but their social existence that determines their consciousness. At a certain stage of development, the material productive forces of society come into conflict with the existing relations of production, or – this merely expresses the same thing in legal terms – with the property relations within the framework of which they have operated hitherto. From forms of development of the productive forces these relations turn into their fetters. Then begins an era of social revolution. With the change of the economic foundations the entire immense superstructure is more or less rapidly transformed. (1975a: 425–6)

For Marx, the primary role of material production, an active relation to the natural world, is an essential fact of human history. Human beings always require food and shelter in order to exist. The ways in which these means of subsistence are produced by individuals and groups working together – 'the social production of their existence' – involves some division of labour and hence some kind of social hierarchy. Since production, work, is so central a part of daily life, social relations involve an active and practical interaction with the material world.

Following from this, these social relations of production and their connected hierarchies, change as the forms of material production change. The relations between forms of material production, the division of labour and social structure – together constituting 'the mode of production' – thus provide a way of thinking about historical change. Periods of development and gradual change are punctuated by periods of crisis, revolution and rapid transformation. These occur when relations of production become incompatible with changing forces of production. They become 'fetters' and are broken open, to be replaced by new relations of production which encourage a further period of development; hence the rise and fall of successive forms of society.

If the social relations of production are underpinned by a dynamic economic structure, they themselves in turn underpin a further set of institutional relations – 'the whole immense superstructure', as he terms it. He distinguishes between 'the material transformation of the economic conditions of production' which can be determined very precisely and 'the legal, political, religious, artistic, or philosophic – in short ideological forms in which men become conscious of this conflict and fight it out' (1975a: 426). The social relations of production change in response to the pressures of the productive forces, and so in turn ideological forms of consciousness have to adapt and change. Moments of crisis, when forces and relations of production are in conflict, will generate conflict within the legal and political superstructure and within consciousness.

It was never, of course, merely 'the economic' as such which was determining. It was always a historically specific matrix of forms of productive activity and social relations which was decisive. Marx insisted that material production must be understood in its specific historical form and not applied as a general category. He commented in the Introduction to the *Grundrisse*:

> There are characteristics which all stages of production have in common, and which are established as general ones by the mind; but the so-called *general preconditions* of all production are nothing more than these abstract moments with which no real historical stage of production can be grasped. (1973c: 88)

This applies equally to the interconnected activities of consumption, distribution and exchange. For instance, in the case of consumption, whatever the historical period, human beings need to provide food and shelter for themselves and their families. But in different periods they go about meeting these needs in different ways. Discussions about basic human needs tend to be abstract – human beings need food, for instance. But the most basic natural human needs are also historically specific and subject to change. Being human itself has a history. As Marx put it in *The Poverty of Philosophy,* 'all history is nothing but a continuous transformation of human nature'. (MECW6: 192). In the *Grundrisse* Marx argues that the need for food is always embedded in a social order which produces particular kinds of foods. People are not simply hungry for 'food'. They are hungry for specific foods produced in a specific time and place: 'Hunger is hunger, but the hunger gratified by cooked meat eaten with a knife and fork is a different hunger from that which bolts down raw meat with the aid of hand, nail and tooth' (1973c: 92).

In a note in the first volume of *Capital* Marx responded to one criticism of the 1859 'Preface' – that the overwhelming centrality of 'the economic' in social life may be applicable to the nineteenth century but not to the ancient world or the medieval period. First, of course, the production of food, shelter, clothing and so on was a precondition of human existence in all periods of history: 'the Middle Ages could not live on Catholicism, nor the ancient world on politics'. But he went on to distinguish between the *determining* role of the economic and the *dominant* role of religion or politics: 'it is the manner in which they gained their livelihood which explains why in one case politics, in the other case Catholicism, played the chief part' (1976: 176n). In *Capital*, and elsewhere, Marx stressed how in pre-capitalist modes of production forms of extra-economic coercion were crucial elements of the social relations of production. In other words, in different forms and at different periods, political structures were constitutive of the economic sphere. A more or less autonomous economic sphere is a distinctive feature of capitalism.

The 1859 'Preface' listed four different modes of production – 'Asiatic, ancient, feudal, and modern bourgeois' – describing them as 'epochs marking progress in the economic development of society' (1975a: 426). So for Marx these modes of production mark an overall increase in the human capacity to exploit the resources of nature and to create societies that were wealthier in terms of material life. Is he, however, proposing an outline of history as a linear and progressive sequence of 'modes of production'? First, sequence of modes of production listed in the 1859 'Preface' and the material on pre-capitalist modes of production in the *Grundrisse* was never treated by Marx and Engels as much more than a working sketch and it was subsequently revised. Nor were these periods, or epochs, water-tight historical compartments. As Marx himself commented in *Capital*: 'We are concerned here only with broad and general characteristics, for epochs in the history of society are no more separated from each other by strict and abstract lines of demarcation than are geological epochs' (1976: 492). Marx and Engels were well aware of the provisional nature of their historical outlines, not least because it was based on limited historical data.[11] More than this, Marx's whole conception of history was antithetical to teleological narratives of historical inevitability with their vocabulary of destiny or their personification of the historical process. *The German Ideology* had already rejected this kind of history as a speculative distortion. It proposed instead a history of generations, each dealing with the resources it inherited and responding to and initiating changes in a fairly ad hoc manner:

> History is nothing but the succession of the separate generations, each of which exploits the materials, the capital funds, the productive forces handed down to it by all preceding generations, and thus, on the one hand, continues the traditional activity in completely changed circumstances and, on the other, modifies the old circumstances with a completely changed activity. (MECW5: 38)

In the notes on 'The Method of Political Economy' which opened *Grundrisse*, Marx was similarly critical of too great a stress on continuity and 'development': 'The so-called historical presentation of development is founded, as a rule, on the fact that the latest form regards the previous ones as steps leading up to itself . . .'. He went on to develop a much more complex understanding of the relationship between the present and the past – one which stressed the 'essential difference' of the past:

> Bourgeois society is the most developed and the most complex historic organization of production. The categories which

> express its relations, the comprehension of its structure, thereby also allows insights into the structure and the relations of production of all the vanished social formations out of whose ruins and elements it built itself up, whose partly still unconquered remnants are carried along within it, whose mere nuances have developed explicit significance within it, etc. Human anatomy contains a key to the anatomy of the ape. The intimations of higher development among the subordinate animal species, however, can be understood only after the higher development is already known. The bourgeois economy thus supplies the key to the ancient, etc. (1973: 105)

Since contemporary capitalism is the most developed and complex social and economic formation, the concepts which both 'express' and 'comprehend' it therefore subsume earlier concepts which expressed and comprehended earlier and simpler societies. But this kind of understanding, Marx hastens to add, is not the same as projecting certain categories and relations specific to existing society back into other historical forms of society. Understanding ground rent helps in understanding tribute, tithe and so on, but these are not the same. The idea that the categories of political economy possess a truth for all other forms of society is, Marx says, 'to be taken only with a grain of salt'. 'They can contain them in a developed, or stunted, or caricatured form etc., but always with an essential difference' (1973: 106). It is the 'essential difference' that is pivotal here. So Marx rejects any method which traces some kind of inevitable line from past to present or posits any kind of *telos* to historical development – or is insensitive to the space between our projections onto the past and the relations and categories of thought of the past itself.

Interestingly, Marx also suggests in this passage, that political economy's understanding was already enhanced by the arguments generated by new socialist currents of thought: 'bourgeois economics arrived at an understanding of feudal, ancient, oriental economics only after the self-criticism of bourgeois society had begun'. In other words, only when political economy's certainties had begun to be undermined by socialist political economy could it begin to see beyond its own historical boundaries. Following on from this, it is also worth noting the important political implication of historicizing the present. Capitalism was just one of a series of modes of production which had emerged, matured and then disintegrated. Slave societies and serf societies had come and gone. So too would societies based upon the exploitation of free labour.

One issue raised in the *Grundrisse* which subsequently generated controversy among Marxists was the existence of a distinctive 'Asiatic' mode of production – one which was represented as essentially cyclical. Without cumulative development it is thus something of a dead-end. This comes dangerously close to some kind of conventional Western ethnocentrism or 'Orientalism' for which the people of the East are a lesser people, lacking the necessary characteristics which make for a dynamic, forward-looking economic and social order. If Marx and Engels initially endorsed the idea of an Asiatic mode of production, they subsequently repudiated it. Engels's remarks in *The Origin of the Family* in 1884 were based upon his close reading of Marx's late notebooks. It reaffirmed the argument that modes of production were defined by their specific forms of exploitation:

> Slavery is the first form of exploitation, the form peculiar to the ancient world; it is succeeded by serfdom in the Middle Ages, and wage labour in the more recent period. These are the three great forms of servitude, characteristic of the three great epochs of civilization.[12]

There was no room here for a distinctive Asiatic form of exploitation, located in 'the East', and thus of an Asiatic mode of production.[13]

HISTORIES

The 1859 'Preface' provides the most succinct summary of the guiding principles of Marx's approach to history. Here in condensed form he summarizes, develops and clarifies some of the central arguments of his earlier writings. He provides a schema for analysing long-term historical change based on the dynamic axis of forces and relations of production. And he provides a model – economic foundation/legal and political superstructure – of the totality of interconnections within a specific historical moment. But this is where the problems begin. What is the theoretical status of these propositions? A number of influential studies have taken this brief text as somehow the ultimate summation of a philosophy of history and the basis for extended book-length discussions of concepts divorced either from the wider body of Marx's work or from much specificity of reference to any real history or even to a world outside the text. This was not how Marx intended the 'Preface' to be read. He was not constructing an authoritative argument about 'History', nor one abstracted out of the rest of his work with its particular focus on the historical dynamics of the present. Note that these enormously influential passages are no more than a few hundred words in a brief preface. 'A few brief remarks regarding the course of my study of political economy' and a 'sketch of the course of my studies' was how Marx described the 1859 Preface (1975b: 424).

If the 1859 'Preface' was a 'sketch' it was also, he observed, 'the result of conscientious investigation lasting many years'. The importance of empirical research and of historical specificity was something Marx and Engels insisted on throughout their career. 'Empirical observation must in each separate instance bring out empirically, and without any mystification and speculation, the connection of the social and political structure with production', *The German Ideology* had stated. This was a point that Engels was forced to repeat again and again in the years after Marx's death as increasing numbers of young disciples seized on 'the economic interpretation of history' as the magic key which opened the door to an understanding of the past. He and Marx, Engels explained to one correspondent, had sometimes overemphasized the importance of the economic:

> Marx and I are ourselves partly to blame for the fact that the younger people sometimes lay more stress on the economic side than is due to it. We had to emphasise the main principle *vis-à-vis* our adversaries, who denied it, and we had not always the time, the place or the opportunity to give their due to the other elements involved in the interaction . . . Unfortunately, however, it happens only too often that people think they have fully understood a new theory and can apply it without more ado from the moment they have assimilated its main principles, and even those not always correctly. And I cannot exempt many of the more recent 'Marxists' from this reproach, for the most amazing rubbish has been produced in this quarter, too . . . (MECW49: 36)

Engels had to repeat this point to recent 'Marxists'. The theoretical schema of 'historical materialism' could not be conjured out of the air by thinking – they required empirical research. And they could not be *applied* in some straightforward manner to individual cases.

Marx's rare general statements about history, part one of *The German Ideology*, some of the introductory sections of *Grundrisse*, a brief passage in the 1859 *Preface* to *A Critique of Political Economy*, have been deservedly influential. But they should not be taken as his final (much less his only) word. As Etienne Balibar has usefully observed: 'These are very general, prospective or summary texts; texts in which the sharpness of the distinctions and the peremptoriness of the claims are only equalled by the brevity of the justifications, the elliptical nature of the definitions.'[14] Such texts need to be read critically and in relation to other texts by Marx – and in particular, the substantial amount of his writing which engages in *concrete analysis*.

CLASS STRUGGLE AND WESTERN MARXISM

Subsequent chapters will explore some important examples of Marx engaging in both theoretical reflection and concrete analysis. But I want to conclude this chapter with an apparent digression. The 1859 'Preface' had emphasized that human history is always a history of the ways in which, through their active relations to their natural and material environment, human beings have created and recreated themselves. It is a history therefore of labour and of production. Because production is a collective activity, this is not a history of particular individuals, of great minds or great artists. Appropriately, it is a *social* history, and therefore in some sense a *democratic* history, since it was about the common or working people who have always made up the vast majority of the peoples of the earth and whose labour created the material foundations of every historical civilization.[15] There is also an important political dimension here. 'The history of all hitherto existing society is the history of class struggles', *The Communist Manifesto* declared in its opening sentence. But the 1859 'Preface' does not mention class struggles, or even class. This was partly to evade the attentions of the Prussian censor. Marx was eager to see the publication of *A Contribution to a Critique of Political Economy* and he had to take care to avoid inflammatory political language and to represent himself as a scholar and a scientific investigator. Thus the preface leaves unexplored some central questions about the dynamic of historical change, underplaying active political agency and overstressing anonymous structural forces.

The history of every mode of production was punctuated by uprisings, rebellions and revolutions of the exploited majority against their oppressors. The *Communist Manifesto* had powerfully represented this long resistance:

> Freeman and slave, patrician and plebeian, lord and serf, guild-master and journeyman, in a word, oppressor and oppressed, stood in constant opposition to one another, carried on an uninterrupted, now hidden, now open fight, a fight that each time ended, either in a revolutionary reconstitution of society at large, or in the common ruin of the contending classes. (2002: 219)

This endless struggle was mostly, at least in the short term, a history of defeat for the productive class. Even so, the working-class movement had a political responsibility to commemorate and to celebrate its defeated forebears. In what Engels many years later described as 'one of his most powerful articles', Marx commented on how the soldiers who were killed during the suppression of the popular uprisings in Paris in June 1848 were honoured and commemorated by the established order: 'the state will look after their widows and orphans, decrees will glorify them, solemn funeral processions will inter their remains, the official press will declare them immortal, the European reaction from east to west will pay homage to them.' For the workers shot down in the streets, however, there were no such official honours:

> [T]he plebeians are tortured with hunger, reviled by the press, abandoned by doctors, abused by honest men as thieves, incendiaries, galley-slaves, their women and children thrown into still deeper misery, their best sons deported overseas: it is the privilege, it is the right of the democratic press to wind the laurels around their stern and threatening brows. (1973: 134)[16]

Marx recognized the political importance of preserving a counter-memory to the official memory of the state with its statues and memorials and official commemorations. 'I know the heroic struggles the English working class have gone through since the middle of the last century – struggles [no] less glorious, because they are shrouded in obscurity, and burked by the middle-class historian,' Marx said in his speech to a gathering of English Chartists in 1856 (1973b: 300). Some elements of this history were to appear in *Capital* – for instance in chapter 10 and the struggle over the length of the working day.

However, recovery of the history of the 'heroic struggles' of the English working class since the middle of the eighteenth century was not something Marx himself pursued. Subsequently, especially in the form of 'History from below', it has become one of the most common ways of doing a Marxist, or at least a socialist history. This became especially influential in Britain the 1960s and 1970s through the work of a group of avowedly Marxist historians.[17] Books like *Society and Puritanism in Pre-Revolutionary England* (1964) and *The World Turned Upside Down* (1972) by Christopher Hill, George Rude's *The Crowd in the French Revolution* (1959) and *Wilkes and Liberty* (1962), Rodney Hilton's *Bond Men Made Free*, Edward Thompson's *The Making of the English Working Class* (1963), Eric Hobsbawm's *Primitive Rebels* (1959) and *Labouring Men* (1964) and *Captain Swing* (1969) co-authored by Hobsbawm and Rude – were of pivotal significance in carving out a space for a new kind of historical writing during the 1960s and 70s. The work of Raphael Samuel and the History Workshop Movement in the 1970s, with its conferences, its journal and its occasional publications, was influential too.[18]

These historians tended to be suspicious of abstract or systematic theories – whether in the form of orthodox Marxism-Leninism, mainstream economic theory or sociology. All three were briskly despatched in Thompson's short preface to *The Making of the English Working Class* in 1963, for instance. The duty of the socialist historian was to bring alive the experiences and the consciousness of working people in the past, to retrieve an alternative people's history and an alternative cultural tradition. Hence their writings were richly textured and densely researched pieces of empirical history. If theories were exploited it was generally as heuristic devices that suggested useful ways of handling empirical data and of retrieving popular consciousness. There was often resistance to structural explanations of one kind or another. It was argued that these depoliticized and de-moralized the past in ways that turned history into an impersonal fate, or an inevitable process, in which popular resistance was a hopeless utopianism at best, a backward-looking irrationalism at worst. The British Marxist Historians, as they are sometimes called, were alert to every trace of mystification in ascribing historical outcomes to inevitability and not to human agency. Their historical writing stressed that poverty and oppression were not inevitable but the consequences of human action. Changes were brought about by men and women acting consciously towards specific purposes. Things could have been different. And the trajectory of English history was in part due to the actions of rebels, utopians, popular radicals – Levellers, Ranters and Diggers, Painites and Luddites, Chartists, trades unionists, and so on. They may have ultimately failed in their aims but they nevertheless changed history for the better.

This concern with reconstructing and validating the mental worlds and the experience and agency of 'the people' finds its exemplary articulation in E. P. Thompson's statement at the beginning of *The Making of the English Working Class.* His aim, he said, was to retrieve the aspirations of those whose values and ways of life were in the process of being wiped out by industrialization:

> I am seeking to rescue the poor stockinger, the Luddite cropper, the'obselete' handloom weaver, the utopian artisan, and even the deluded follower of Joanna Southcott, from the enormous condescension of posterity. Their crafts and traditions may have been dying. Their hostility to the new industrialism may have been backward-looking. Their communitarian ideals may have been fantasies. Their insurrectionary conspiracies may have been foolhardy. But they lived through these times of acute social disturbance, and we did not.[19]

This kind of emphasis reappears throughout the writing of this generation of Marxist historians in Britain. It is there, for instance, in George Rude's comment that to understand popular movements and crowd actions it is necessary not just to understand precisely who was involved, whose were the faces in the crowd, but also to 'get into the skulls of the participants', to understand their perceptions of the situation, their motives and their values, no matter how different from our own.[20] It is also there in Christopher Hill's concern with the consciousness and the experience of all kinds of radical seventeenth-century writers and preachers, though their religious language is so alien to the concerns of the modern secular historian.[21]

For these historians, understanding of the past has to confront the apparent irrationalities of the common people and cannot restrict itself to the coherent writings of an educated elite. It must confront the specificities of popular and everyday experience. It must identify with the exploited, the oppressed, the marginal in order to recover and revalidate a history of popular resistance. And this had directly political implications. 'The Jacobins are still alive in France today: not the Levellers in England', Hill remarks.[22] The role of the socialist historian was to restore to popular memory and to the labour movement struggles and aspirations and ideas which had been concealed and forgotten by official history.

There are important convergences between the so-called 'British Marxist Historians' and the various schools of Western Marxism that circulated in Europe and elsewhere, especially from the 1950s. This is too large and complex a topic to pursue in any depth. However I want to look briefly at one key figure in this Western Marxism – Jean-Paul Sartre – and his reading of Marx in his *Search for a Method*, first published in 1960.[23] For most contemporary Marxists in the 1950s – 'Stalinist Marxism', as Sartre sometimes called it – History was represented as an immanent force and men were merely its puppets. This was, he says, 'a dialectic without men'. It was itself the product of a history. The ebbing away of the revolutionary energies that swept Europe after the end of the First World War, left Soviet Marxism encircled and isolated. Unity and conformity to the requirements of the party became more important than any process of open debate, self-criticism and theoretical development. As a result, the open-ended categories of Marx, developed to guide empirical research and focus debate, were transformed into closed doctrines and timeless truths, administered by a bureaucratic and conservative party elite. 'For years the Marxist intellectual believed that he served his party by violating experience, by overlooking embarrassing details, by grossly simplifying the data, and above all, by conceptualizing the event *before* having studied it' (23). This kind of *a priori* Marxism, Sartre complained, always knows the answer to any question without requiring further investigation:

> It does not derive its concepts from experience – or at least not from the new experiences which it seeks to interpret. It has already formed its concepts; it is already certain of their truth;

> it will assign to them the role of constitutive schemata. Its sole purpose is to force the events, the persons, or the acts considered into prefabricated molds. (37)

Though Sartre never denies the influence of conditions, he insists – and claims that he is following Marx in this – that it is men who make history. One of the fundamental characteristics of man is his ability to go beyond his situation. He is never identical with it, but exists in an active and changing relation to it. Thus *he* determines how he will himself live his situation and what its meaning is to be. This is the core of Sartre's existentialism, but now developed through his engagement with Marx and Marxism. Men make history by this continual surpassing of the particular conditions which constitute the specific situation they find themselves in. Human events are not pre-determined. For Sartre there is no immanent law, no hyperorganism controlling men's relations with one another.

When Sartre looks closely at Marx's historical writings on the revolution of 1848 in France he finds that events are never fitted into some *a priori* historical schema. A contemporary French Marxist, Sartre says, would probably subsume the tragic history of the French republic of 1848 into a simple political lesson: the proletariat was betrayed by its ally the republican petite bourgeoisie. This is not what Marx does. He engages in a detailed empirical investigation into the political processes involved:

> Thus living Marxism is heuristic; its principles and its prior knowledge appear as regulative in relation to its concrete research. In the work of Marx we never find entities. Totalities (e.g., 'the petite bourgeoisie' of the 18 Brumaire) are living; they furnish their own definitions within the framework of the research. (26)

In other words, in any historical situation attention has to be paid to the historically specific characteristics of an entity such as the petite bourgeoisie which make it always a unique reality. In a detailed discussion of the French Revolution, Sartre is keen to stresses the irreducibility of political reality and the importance of focusing on real men in their precise situations: 'the rapid, schematic explanation of the war as an operation of the commercial bourgeoisie causes those men whom we know well to disappear – Brissot, Guadet, Gensonne,

Vergniaud – or else it constitutes them, in the final analysis, as the purely passive instruments of their class' (44). A rigid and mechanistic Marxism reduces complex realities to simple abstractions. But for Sartre – as for Marx – it is never 'the economy' or 'class' or 'imperialism' which is determining but always much more complex combinations: 'men, their objectifications and their labors, human relations, are finally what is most concrete' (50). Concepts and arguments developed by Marx are, Sartre says, guiding principles and indications of work that needs to be done – work that requires detailed and critical investigation of a range of sources of evidence.

This brings us back precisely to Engels and his critical remarks on the dangers of constructing an abstract philosophy of history out of Marx's writings. As he put it succinctly to one correspondent: 'the materialist method turns into its opposite if it is not taken as one's guiding principle in historical investigation but as a ready-made pattern to which one shapes the facts of history to suit oneself' (1975b: 390–1). And a few years later Marx contrasted how the dispossession of the free peasants of ancient Rome gave rise not, as in the English case, to capitalism but to slavery:

> Thus events strikingly analogous but taking place in different historical surroundings led to totally different results. By studying each of these forms of evolution separately and then comparing them one can easily find the clue to this phenomenon, but one will never arrive there by using as one's master key a general historico-philosophical theory, the supreme virtue of which consists in being supra-historical. (1975b: 294)

With this stress on historical specificity we must now turn to the pages of *Capital*.

CHAPTER 4

POLITICAL ECONOMY AND THE HISTORY OF CAPITALISM

> *. . . in the analysis of economic forms neither microscopes nor chemical reagents are of assistance. The power of abstraction must replace both.*
>
> (1976: 90)

> *Centuries are required before the 'free' labourer, owing to the greater development of the capitalist mode of production, makes a voluntary agreement, i.e., is compelled by social conditions to sell the whole of his active life, his very capacity for labour, in return for the price of his customary means of subsistence, to sell his birthright for a mess of pottage.*
>
> (1976: 382)

> *Just as man is governed, in religion, by the products of his own brain, so, in capitalist production, he is governed by the products of his own hand.*
>
> (1976: 772)

POLITICAL ECONOMY

At first glance at its contents page, the first volume of *Capital* – the summa of Marx's effort to produce an effective *critique* of political economy – does look remarkably like a work of political economy itself:

Part I: Commodities and Money
1: Commodities

2: Exchange
3: Money, or the Circulation of Commodities
Part II: The Transformation of Money in Capital
4: The General Formula for Capital
5: Contradictions in the General Formula of Capital
6: The Buying and Selling of Labour-Power.

And so on. Frequently in *Capital*, for the sake of exposition, Marx utilizes the kind of simple abstract economic models which political economists use. He posits a pure capitalism of capitalists and workers relating to each other in a simple production process, disregarding, as he put it, 'all phenomena that conceal the workings of its inner mechanism' (1976: 710). In Part I of *Capital* he explains in a simple narrative how money is turned into capital through a combination of means of production, raw materials and labour power. Brought together in the production process the result is a supply of commodities which is then turned into a sum of money greater than the original capital. Hence the origin of surplus value, which is demonstrated, via this simple model, to be unpaid labour: 'the capitalist always makes labour-power work longer than is necessary for the reproduction of its own value'.

Such 'analytical fictions' are part of Marx's exposition for the reader of some basic principles. These are subsequently developed in much more complex and precisely focused arguments in which Marx moves from ideal model to concrete analysis, introducing a political and historical dynamic. *Capital* was subtitled 'A Critique of Political Economy'. The term 'critique' alluded to Immanuel Kant's *Critique of Pure Reason* and its demolition of the theoretical pretensions of reason to reach any kind of certainty. Marx was similarly engaged in a *critique* of political economy to demonstrate the falsity of its claims to provide ultimate and permanent truths. But for Marx an adequate 'critique' was not just destructive. It had also to demonstrate the origin and the significance of these false claims. For instance, in the *Critique of Hegel's Philosophy of Right*, Marx argued that it was insufficient merely to point to the contradictions of the political constitution: 'true philosophical criticism of the present state constitution not only shows the contradictions as existing, but clarifies them, grasps their essence and necessity. It comprehends their own proper significance' (MECW3: 5). In other words, the task of critique was to show not just that something was false but also how it was, in certain respects, true too – or, at least, made some kind of sense.

Why was political economy so important for Marx to critique? First, the concerns of classical political economy were much wider than the curriculum of 'Economics' in most universities today. Much more than a technical study of a number of discrete and specific 'economic' issues, political economy was an often eclectic and wide-ranging political, social and historical theory. Adam Smith's *The Wealth of Nations* was one of its founding texts – one that Marx never ceased to read. It includes chapters on the division of labour, wages, money, prices, rent and so on.[1] But there is also much material which is philosophical, political, historical and even sociological. Classical political economy also provided practical guidance in the conduct of government policy on a wide range of issues. It was, in Smith's words, 'the science of a statesman or legislator'. And this is a second key point about political economy. It was the most powerful social theory of Marx's day. Its influence radiated throughout English and increasingly European and North American society. It possessed, despite a good deal of opposition, considerable intellectual authority. It shaped the policies of governments, especially policy towards the poor. It influenced how employers ran their businesses. It infiltrated the language and common sense of the period. Ebenezer Scrooge in Charles Dickens' novel *Christmas Carol* is one embodiment of the spirit of Victorian political economy.[2]

Third, and most important, political economy was an expression of some of the central structures of contemporary society. There is an important section of the *Grundrisse*, 'The Method of Political Economy', in which Marx reflects on political economy and the relationship between the abstract and the concrete, between concepts and concrete realities. How, he asks, do we begin to consider a given country 'politico-economically'? 'It seems to be correct to begin with the real and the concrete, with the real precondition, thus to begin, in economics, with e.g. the population, which is the foundation and the subject of the entire social act of production' (1973: 100). However, if we examine this proposition more closely, he says, we find that this is false. Starting with the population is to start with an empty abstraction if we don't ask further questions – about how the population is divided up into social classes, for instance. These classes, in turn, remain nothing but empty terms unless there is some understanding of wage labour and capital in that country, which in turns requires some grasp of the division of labour, of exchange and prices, and so on. As the starting-place for any understanding of a particular country, the population, as such, would be 'a chaotic conception', Marx says. It would lead by further analysis 'from the imagined concrete towards ever thinner abstractions' until arriving at 'the simplest determinations'. This is how early political economy proceeded, concluding with 'a small number of determinant, abstract, general relations such as division of labour, money, value, etc.'.

On the other hand, Marx suggests, it was possible to move from these kinds of simple relations – labour, division of labour, exchange and so on – back by a reverse journey to the concrete, through detailed research and through critical use of concepts, 'until I had finally arrived at the population again, but this time not as the chaotic conception of a whole, but as a rich totality of many determinations and relations'. So, the concrete is not the same as the empirical object – the given country which he wants to provide a 'politico-economic' account of. But nor is it on the other hand, as Hegel had proposed, the result of thought itself. It is impossible to deduce the concrete either from concepts or from empirical data. 'The concrete is concrete because it is the concentration of many determinations', Marx says (1973: 101). It is both the point of departure and the point of arrival of the analysis but the journey between requires critical thinking and a dialogue between concepts and empirical materials. As Marx commented in the preface to *Capital*: 'in the analysis of economic forms neither microscopes nor chemical reagents are of assistance. The power of abstraction must replace both' (1976: 90). In other words, we must abstract in thought the various determinations – conceptual, ideological, empirical – which are concentrated in the concrete object of analysis, since we cannot isolate them experimentally in a way that a chemist could. The 'power of abstraction' is the capacity to work critically with these determinations and their relations – to think critically about the limitations of a concept or of particular empirical data.

Marx placed considerable weight on the value of the categories of political economy, critically appropriated, for an understanding of the present because they arise out of a critical dialogue between concepts and practices and structures – and thus out of the concrete realities of bourgeois society. In the work of certain key figures such as Adam Smith and Ricardo, they provide knowledge and a basis for further investigation of 'bourgeois society':

> [E]ven the most abstract categories, despite their validity – precisely because of their abstractness – for all epochs, are nevertheless, in the specific character of this abstraction, themselves likewise a product of historic relations, and possess their full validity only for and within these relations. (1973c: 105)

Marx's long and arduous exploration of bourgeois political economy was because its basic concepts and categories were, as he put it, 'forms of thought which are socially valid, and therefore objective, for the relations of production belonging to the historically determined mode of social production, i.e., commodity production' (1976: 169). In other words, classical political economy was, in its own historical moment, 'true'. It provided elements of a scientific analysis of the workings of capitalist society, and Marx's own counter-analysis had to begin with it: 'the first criticism of any science is necessarily influenced by the premises of the science it is fighting against' (MECW4: 31).

Political economy is the essential *starting place* for Marx. But it is not where his intellectual journey ends. Again we should remember the title of his great work: *Capital: A Critique of Political Economy*. Marx distinguished between a political economy which had scientific value because it 'investigated the real relations of production in bourgeois society', and, on the other hand, 'vulgar political economy' which dealt merely with appearances and was little more than the expression of particular social and economic interests. For Marx, David Ricardo was the last great representative of political economy as a genuinely critical and scientific project to understand the real world. By making 'the antagonism of class-interests, of wages and profits, of profits and rent, the starting point of his investigations', he provided genuine insights into the economic and social realities of early-nineteenth-century England. But, presupposing capitalism as 'the absolutely final form of social production, instead of as a passing historical phase of its evolution', political economy could preserve its limited scientific value only so long as the antagonism of capital and labour was relatively undeveloped. After 1830, as the bourgeoisie began to consolidate its political power and to assert its claims to represent the 'interest' of society as a whole, it confronted an increasingly organized working class which was challenging these claims. In place of 'genuine scientific research', political economy became more and more a matter of defending particular economic and social interests.

> It was thenceforth no longer a question whether this or that theorem was true, but whether it was useful to capital or harmful, expedient or inexpedient, in accordance with police regulations or contrary to them. In place of disinterested inquirers there stepped hired prize fighters; in place of genuine scientific research, the bad conscience and the evil intent of apologetics. (1976: 97)

A few political economists, Marx says, 'still claimed some scientific standing and aspired to be something more than mere sophists and sycophants of the ruling-classes'; he mentions John Stuart Mill. But their attempts 'to harmonise the Political Economy of capital with the claims, no longer to be ignored, of the proletariat' were, he said, 'a declaration of bankruptcy' (1976: 98).

Locked within their own conceptual boundaries, political economists view the capitalist order as 'the absolute and ultimate form of social production, instead of as a historically transient stage of development' (1976: 96). Political economy thus expressed the relations of bourgeois production, the division of labor, credit, money and so on, as fixed, immutable, eternal categories. This failure of historical perspective remained one of Marx's constant and basic criticisms of political economy. In one of his earliest forays into political economy, *The Poverty of Philosophy*, Marx argued that economic categories like rent, profit, wages, money, competition and so on are 'abstractions of actual social relations that are transitory and historical'. A French socialist like Proudhon was as blind to this as any political economist, Marx explained:

> He fails to see that *economic categories* are but *abstractions* of those real relations, that they are truths only in so far as those relations continue to exist. Thus he falls into the error of bourgeois economists who regard those economic categories as eternal laws and not as historical laws which are laws only for a given historical development, a specific development of the productive forces. (MECW38: 95)

For instance, for political economy capital was simply a set of things – raw materials, tools and machinery, money, and so on. For Marx this is too narrow and technical a description. For him, capital is 'a social relation of production' – it involves the power for some people to control and use the labour of other people and to appropriate a share of what their labour produces. Raw materials, tools, money are not in themselves capital. They become capital only in a specific social situation – one in which there are significant numbers of people who have no way of producing their own subsistence. Capital can only spring into life, Marx says, 'when the owner of the means of production and subsistence meets in the market with the free labourer selling his labour-power'.

The owner of capital and the political economist have no interest in why this situation exists. For them, the labour market is simply a given – one market among others. Marx found a droll lesson of the consequences of this kind of historical blindness in the story of Thomas Peel, who took with him from England to Swan River in Western Australia, means of subsistence and of production to the amount of £50,000 as well as 300 working-class men, women, and children. But, soon after arriving, these working people saw that they could live independently in Australia and deserted their employer. As Edward Gibbon Wakefield complained:

> Where land is very cheap and all men are free, where every one who so pleases can easily obtain a piece of land for himself, not only is labour very dear, as respects the labourer's share of the produce, but the difficulty is to obtain combined labour at any price. (quoted 1976: 934–5)

The result: 'Mr. Peel was left without a servant to make his bed or fetch him water from the river'. Marx comments in a brilliant wisecrack: 'Unhappy Mr. Peel who provided for everything except the export of English relations of production to Swan River!'(1976: 933). So, Marx demonstrates what he means when he says that capital is a social relation:

> Wakefield discovered that, in the colonies, property in money, means of subsistence, machines, and other means of production does not as yet stamp a man as a capitalist if the essential complement to these things is missing: the wage-labourer, the

> other man, who is compelled to sell himself of his own free-will. He discovered that capital is not a thing, but a social relation between persons which is mediated through things. (1976: 932)

In the *Communist Manifesto* there is a discussion of property which again demonstrates the limitations of political economy – and further clarifies what it means to say that capital is a social relation. To the objection that the Communists wanted to abolish property, Marx responded that the status of property has been subject to change throughout history. The French Revolution had abolished such feudal property as survived in 1789, for instance. 'The distinguishing feature of communism is not the abolition of property generally, but the abolition of bourgeois property' (2002: 235). This latter form of property, he went on, is not that personal property which is 'the fruit of a man's own labour'. The property of the petty artisan or the small peasant did, to some extent, answer to such a description. But, Marx drily observes, the Communists had no need to abolish it: 'the development of industry has to a great extent already destroyed it, and is still destroying it daily'. Bourgeois property is something very different. Owning a cotton factory or a shipyard or a warehouse or a substantial sum of money is not the same as owning a hat, a coat or a book. Personal possessions and capital are very different things. 'Capital is a collective product', but it is privately appropriated by a minority and then used as an instrument of power to extract further surplus value from the labour-power of others. Capital is a social relationship rooted in exploitation of, and domination over, labour. What communists intend to abolish is this particular social form of property – bourgeois property, which is the illegitimate power of a minority over this collective product.

> When, therefore, capital is converted into common property, into the property of all members of society, personal property is not thereby transformed into social property. It is only the social character of the property that is changed. It loses its class character. (2002: 236)

Material objects only become private property because of a whole network of values, ideologies and institutions which are the result of complex historical processes – and which involve power. Private property itself is a political institution.

This political history concealed inside 'the economic' is at the heart of Marx's critique of political economy and of his passionate commitment to the revolutionary transformation of the profoundly unequal and unjust social order which political economy represented and justified. On the one hand, it is obvious where the wages of labourers come from. They perform long hours of labour and in return receive a specified sum of money – wages. But bourgeois property owners draw an income without apparently engaging in much, if any, productive activity. Where does this income – variously called rent, profit, interest – originate? This is a large and complex question, but essentially Marx's argument is that these apparently distinct sources of income are merely forms of the 'surplus value' that owners of capital, directly or indirectly, generate out of the purchase of labour power. The industrial capitalist, running a factory, is visibly drawing an income from a specific enterprise. The City banker or the broker or the merchant, though not directly involved in production, perform definite functions in the circulation of capital and in the distribution of the 'surplus value' generated at the point of production. Even the gentleman living on his portfolio of investments or the landowner living on his rental income are living on the surplus extracted from labour, though at several removes.

Capital does not of itself generate income. A pile of money in a bank vault gathers dust but it does not increase. It has to be invested in some kind of enterprise which will generate surplus value and thus increase the sum invested:

> Capital, therefore, is not only the command over labour, as Adam Smith thought. It is essentially the command over unpaid labour. All surplus-value, whatever particular form (profit, interest, or rent) it may subsequently crystallize into, is in substance the materialization of unpaid labour-time. The secret of the self-valorization of capital resolves itself into the fact that it has at its disposal a definite quantity of the unpaid labour of other people. (1976: 672)

In other words, the labourer is paid less than the value of the labour he or she has actually performed and certain other people trouser the difference. This is what Marx means by the term 'exploitation'. Surplus value is essentially unpaid labour. In effect, and to put it at its simplest, the worker produces after a certain number of hours of labour the value for which he is paid by the employer. He then works additional hours for which he is not paid. Or, to put it another way, what a worker earns in a week is less than the value of his labour to his employer. There is no need to follow Marx into the long and complicated analyses of his labour theory of value to grasp this central and observable fact – that some people work for wages, that others do not and live from various sources of unearned income. How does this odd situation come about and how does it persist? What is the source of the ability of this minority to appropriate a surplus out of the labour of the majority?

It could be argued that these are not 'economic' questions at all but political questions – that the language of political economy is merely a mystification of what is fundamentally a question of power. There is no institution of the capitalist economy which is not also a political institution reproducing the essential relationship of exploitation at the heart of the labour process. The appropriation of unpaid labour by an elite of property owners is supported and maintained by the state, by the legal system, and by a network of organizations and institutions and discourses. Force is another dimension of the state's involvement in the maintenance and reproduction of the relationship between capital and labour. However, force is not a permanent necessity. This is a cardinal point for Marx and it differentiates capitalism from other modes of production. Though in contemporary capitalism relations of production are also relations of *domination*, they reproduce themselves via 'the silent compulsion of economic relations':

> The advance of capitalist production develops a working class which by education, training and habit looks upon the requirement of that mode of production as self-evident natural laws. The organisation of the capitalist process of production, once it is fully developed, breaks down all resistance. The constant generation of a relative surplus population keeps the law of supply and demand of labour, and therefore wages, within *narrow* limits which correspond to capital's valorisation requirements. The silent compulsion of economic relations sets the seal on the domination of the capitalist over the worker. Direct extra-economic force is still of course used, but only in exceptional cases. In the ordinary run of things, the worker can be left to the 'natural laws

> of production', i.e. it is possible to rely on his dependence on capital, which springs from the conditions of production themselves and is guaranteed in perpetuity by them. (1976: 899)

In other words, the political content of economic relations is obscured by the reality of everyday life. Capitalist production, Marx says, 'of itself' reproduces the separation between labour-power and the means of labour and thus the dependency of the worker upon wage-labour. 'It incessantly forces him to sell his labour-power in order to live, and enables the capitalist to purchase labour-power in order that he may enrich himself.' The 'silent compulsion' of how things are becomes a kind of natural order. But of course there is nothing natural about it. It has historical origins and is in process of continuous change.

Before coming to the historical preconditions of capitalism it is worth briefly exploring one dimension of that 'silent compulsion of economic relations' which completes the domination of the capitalist over the worker. *Capital* begins with the commodity. Material objects produced by human labour for use are transformed into commodities which can be exchanged on the basis of a quantitative measure of their exchange value: a bunch of red grapes costs about 10 per cent of a book which costs about 10 per cent of a warm overcoat. These very particular material objects – grapes, a book, a coat – share nothing except that they can be measured against each other on a single grid of prices. And this grid of equivalences enables anything to be exchanged for anything else. Exchange value thus abstracts from the use-value of an object and from all of its material characteristics:

> It is no longer a table, a house, a piece of yarn or any other useful thing. All its sensuous characteristics are extinguished. Nor is it any longer the product of the labour of the joiner, the mason or the spinner, or of any other kind of productive labour. With the disappearance of the useful character of the products of labour, the useful character of the various kinds of labour embodied in them also disappears; this in turn entails the disappearance of the different concrete forms of labour. (1976: 128)

There are a whole set of economic questions about value which Marx pursues in detail but the key issue here is taken up in the fourth section of chapter 1: 'The Fetishism of the Commodity and its

Secret'. Marx points out how the system of commodity production is obscure. On the one hand it is a complex social system through which, via the division of labour, people depend on each other for their necessities. The baker depends upon the butcher for his meat; the butcher depends upon the baker to produce his bread. However, they are strangers to each other – their only relationship to each other is via the buying and selling of the goods they produce. The labour of different individuals are connected not by social relations between them but by the buying and selling of things; as Marx succinctly puts it, 'they do not appear as direct social relations between persons in their work, but rather as material relations between persons and social relations between things' (1976: 166). Value seems to be inherent in the objects that are for sale and the concrete labour of real people who produced them disappears. This transfer of social properties onto material things is, for Marx, a kind of 'fetishism'. In the same way the capacity to generate interest seems to be a natural property of capital. What is in reality a complex structure of social relations predicated on power and exploitation appears on the surface of everyday life in the form of the market as something which is natural, fair, equal and inevitable.

'PRIMITIVE ACCUMULATION'

How did there come to exist a large population of the propertyless, needing to sell their labour-power? And how did there come to exist an elite of capitalists with control of the means of production – and of much else? Two complementary histories begin to provide answers to these questions, making up major sections of the first volume of *Capital*. The first is the history of 'so-called primitive accumulation', the long process which created the modern free labourer. The second is the history of the transformation of the labour process, culminating in mechanization – the so-called 'industrial revolution'. The first history corresponds very much to the sphere of circulation, the noisy public world of the free market, where the sale and purchase of labour-power goes on. The latter is a history of the hidden world of production.

As the unfortunate Mr Peel discovered in Australia, a workforce without land or other kinds of property is the necessary precondition for a capitalist society. The capitalist must find the free labourer on hand in the market – free in the sense that he is not a slave or a serf or any kind of bondsman and so can dispose of his labour-power as his own 'commodity' however he chooses. But, the labourer must be free in another sense – free as in available and, in effect, unemployed and needing employment. She sells her labour-power because she has no other commodity for sale, no money and no access to materials or means of production by which she could realize her own labour-power in the form of food, clothing and shelter:

> . . . nature does not produce on the one side owners of money or commodities, and on the other hand men possessing nothing but their own labour-power. This relation has no basis in natural history, nor does it have a social basis common to all periods of human history. It is clearly the result of a past historical development, the product of many economic revolutions, of the extinction of a whole series of older formations of social production. (1976: 273)

According to Marx, 'the real science of political economy ends by regarding the bourgeois production relations as merely *historical* ones'. From this moment, 'the delusion' of regarding the capitalist mode of production as the 'natural', and thus final, economic structure disappears. To historicize is always to denaturalize – to point out that what *is* was different in the past and therefore can be different again. The labour market is an institution made by human beings and therefore it can be changed, reformed or even abolished. To historicize therefore always has political ramifications.

Chapters 26–33 of the first volume of *Capital* use the historical case of Britain between the fifteenth and the eighteenth centuries and the concept of 'primitive accumulation' to explain how 'free labour' came to be there, crowding the labour market of mid-Victorian England. These chapters provide both a critique of political economy for its theoretical and historical limitations and an exposure of the systematic distortions of the historical record in dominant perspectives on past and present. Contemporary explanations of why there existed elite of landowners and a large majority of propertyless labourers fell back on myths which legitimized the status quo. Here is Marx's sardonic outline of the moral fable of why there were rich and poor in contemporary Britain:

> Long, long ago there were two sorts of people; one, the diligent, intelligent, and, above all, frugal elite; the other, lazy rascals,

> spending their substance, and more, in riotous living. The legend of theological original sin tells us certainly how man came to be condemned to eat his bread in the sweat of his brow; but the history of economic original sin reveals to us that there are people to whom this is by no means essential. Never mind! Thus it came to pass that the former sort accumulated wealth, and the latter sort finally had nothing to sell except their own skins. And from this original sin dates the poverty of the great majority who, despite all their labour, have up to now nothing to sell but themselves, and the wealth of the few that increases constantly, although they have long ceased to work. (1976: 873)

This narrative of primitive accumulation, Marx says, plays the same role in political economy as original sin does in Christian theology. Except that, for one small section of society in this particular theology there is no original sin and no expulsion from Eden into a world where man is 'condemned to eat his bread in the sweat of his brow'. 'In the tender annals of Political Economy', Marx comments, 'the idyllic reigns from time immemorial'.

Marx is scathing about such fairy stories of how modern capital originated in virtue, hard work and frugal living. Instead he outlines a counter-history of the present – one which stresses that what is at issue here is not merely an accumulation over time of wealth and property by some individuals but a radical redistribution of wealth and a massive transformation of social relations. This is why he refers to it as 'so-called primitive accumulation' – 'so-called', because what is involved is not merely the addition of material objects. 'Primitive accumulation' is, Marx says, 'nothing else than the historical process of divorcing the producer from the means of production' (1976: 875). The genesis of capitalism required the uprooting of labour from the land and the natural environment. A long and complex process transformed serfs and feudal retainers into peasants and finally into landless labourers, deprived of access to the products of nature and so deprived of their own means of production (food, wood for fires, shelter, raw materials and so on). Forced to work for a wage or starve they became 'free' labourers. Marx investigates this process as it worked itself out in Britain. The disappearance of serfdom by the end of the fourteenth century generated a population of free peasant proprietors. During the fifteenth and sixteenth century many of these were thrown onto the labour market, a process accelerated by the protestant reformation and the 'privatisation' of the estates of the largest landowner of all, the Church of Rome. The yeomanry, the class of independent owner-occupiers, farming their own land, was still the backbone of Cromwellian England. Over the following century, however, there was a marked shift of property away from the yeomanry and lesser gentry and towards the large landowners. At the same time the enclosure movement and a whole body of laws excluded the growing numbers of landless labourers from access to the commons which was essential for their subsistence. Millions of acres of common fields and commons were taken into private hands by enclosure acts passed through a parliament of landlords in what was simply legalized robbery. The most blatant examples of the wholesale expropriation of land and natural resources from rural populations occurred in Scotland and Ireland in the form of 'the clearances', by which numerous villages and communities were brutally swept away.

Marx summarizes what he describes as a 'whole series of thefts, outrages, and popular misery, that accompanied the forcible expropriation of the people, from the last third of the 15th to the end of the 18th century':

> The spoliation of the Church's property, the fraudulent alienation of the state domains, the theft of the common lands, the usurpation of feudal and clan property and its transformation into modern private property under circumstances of ruthless terrorism, all these things were just so many idyllic methods of primitive accumulation. They conquered the field for capitalist agriculture, incorporated the soil into capital, and created for the urban industries the necessary supplies of free and rightless proletarians. (1976: 895)

Marx's next chapter looks at legislation through which these supplies of labour were disciplined into freedom. Those who could not be absorbed by the labour market became 'beggars, robbers and vagabonds, partly from inclination, in most cases under the force of circumstances'. Yet the law treated all of them as 'voluntary criminals'. At the same time wage levels were eroded as traditional forms of legal protection for labour were removed. The historical genesis of free labour, then, required the disciplinary power of the state. Laws and courts and prisons were instruments for the dispossession of the peasants, the brutal disciplining of labour and the prevention, by violence if necessary, of any collective organization to resist this. The English Parliament, Marx says, 'held the position of a permanent trade union of the capitalists against the workers throughout five centuries' (1976: 903). Primitive accumulation, the process which dispossessed the English yeomanry and created 'free labour', also produced the great landowner, the capitalist farmer, the home market for industrial capital, and ultimately, the industrial capitalist. Marx had made this point succinctly in the pages of *Grundrisse*:

> The history of landed property, which would demonstrate the gradual transformation of the feudal landlord into the landowner, of the hereditary, semitributary and often unfree tenant for life into the modern farmer, and of the resident serfs, bondsmen and villeins who belonged to the property into agricultural day-labourers, would indeed be the history of the formation of modern capital. (1973c: 252–3)

Keith Wrightson, has recently commented on Marx's solid grounding in the historical sources of this period and in the arguments of the powerful Scottish historical school, represented by Adam Smith and John Millar: 'Far from being an alien intruder upon the interpretation of Britain's economic past, as he is sometimes represented, Marx's ideas and arguments place him firmly in a line of descent that can be traced back to the sixteenth century itself.'[3] And another important historian of early-modern Britain, Peter Linebaugh has recently referred to Marx as 'a British social historian', provoking us to think in new ways about what he was doing in the pages of *Capital*.[4] However, though Marx does broach here some of the key issues which any such history would need to investigate, he is not concerned in these pages to write a history of Britain between the fifteenth- and the late eighteenth century.[5] He is doing both less and more than that. Instead he is interested in the genealogy of the present and, in particular, the genealogy of free labour and of capital. Marx's question is: how did things get to be the way they are? Even a critical reading of political economy, if it remains locked within its ahistorical conceptual framework, has no answer to this question:

> We have seen how money is transformed into capital; how surplus-value is made through capital, and how more capital is

> made from surplus-value. But the accumulation of capital presupposes surplus-value; surplus-value presupposes capitalist production; capitalist production presupposes the availability of considerable masses of capital and labour-power in the hands of commodity producers. The whole movement, therefore, seems to turn around in a never-ending circle which we can only get out of by assuming a primitive accumulation . . . which precedes capitalist accumulation; an accumulation which is not the result of the capitalist mode of production but its point of departure. (1976: 873)

The British case is taken to be an exemplar of a more general process of the development of the preconditions for capitalist production. Following on from this, Marx's genealogy has a critical function. It explodes the claims of contemporary owners of capital that their land, estates, property originated in the moral virtue and hard work of their forebears. It also reveals the brutal economic and social realities obscured by liberal histories of progress: 'the historical movement which changes the producers into wage-workers, appears, on the one hand, as their emancipation from serfdom and from the fetters of the guilds, and this side alone exists for our bourgeois historians.' But the other untold history is one of expropriation: 'these new freedmen became sellers of themselves only after they had been robbed of all their own means of production, and of all the guarantees of existence afforded by the old feudal arrangements' (1976: 875). Marx's account of primitive accumulation, though it is about land and labour and production and about the social origins of the labourer, the farmer and the landowner, is fundamentally political. The historical record was, Marx said, 'written in the annals of mankind in letters of blood and fire', involving generations of systematic state violence and of the appropriation of natural resources into the hands of the few. 'So-called primitive accumulation' is, at one and the same time, an economic, social and political concept.

This is even more pronounced if we focus on another dimension of 'so-called primitive accumulation' – the appropriation of natural resources and the dispossession of people across the planet:

> The discovery of gold and silver in America, the extirpation, enslavement and entombment in mines of the indigenous population of that continent, the beginnings of the conquest and

> plunder of India, the conversion of Africa into a preserve for the commercial hunting of black-skins, are all things which characterize the dawn of the era of capitalist production. These idyllic proceedings are the chief moments of primitive accumulation. (1976: 915)

Spain, Portugal, France and Holland were all involved in these kinds of appropriations in the extra-European world. But it is in England at the end of the seventeenth century, Marx argues, that the key organizational elements of a new system – colonies, the national debt, modern forms of taxation and the protectionist system – were brought together. It is important to stress again, as Marx does, that this combination required force and political will:

> These methods depend in part on brute force, for instance the colonial system. But they all employ the power of the State, the concentrated and organized force of society, to hasten, as in a hothouse, the process of transformation of the feudal mode of production into the capitalist mode, and to shorten the transition. Force is the midwife of every old society which is pregnant with a new one. It is itself an economic power. (1976: 915–16)

The colonial system was crucial for the development of capitalism. It monopolized huge markets for the emerging manufactures of Europe and thus generated an increased accumulation of capital. At the same time and more directly, in Marx's words: 'The treasures captured outside Europe by undisguised looting, enslavement and murder flowed back to the mother-country and were turned into capital there' (1976: 918).

Marx proceeds to explore how the national debt and the development of an international system of credit were vital levers of primitive accumulation in the seventeenth and eighteenth centuries. Just as the 'the villainies of the Venetian system of robbery formed one of the secret foundations of Holland's wealth in capital', so by the eighteenth century Dutch capital found its way into the English capital market. But just in case the reader was beginning to think that this was about flows of capital in some kind of detached financial space, Marx brings us back to the human consequences of accumulation. It is rooted in the appropriation of resources out of the hands of those who labour, including labouring children, and into the hands of those who own capital. 'A great deal of capital, which appears to-day in the United States without any birth-certificate, was yesterday, in England, the capitalized blood of children' (1976: 920). This period of 'so-called primitive accumulation' was also characterized by protectionism and by bitter commercial wars and the brutal destruction of manufacturing in dependent territories wherever it threatened the interests of home production – for instance the Irish woollen manufacture.

Slavery and the slave trade, the colonial system, rising public debts, heavy taxes, protectionism and commercial wars – these, Marx says, were 'children of the true manufacturing period'. At the same, he went on, 'the public opinion of Europe had lost the last remnant of shame and conscience. The nations bragged cynically of every infamy that served them as a means to capitalistic accumulation'. Capital, he says, 'comes dripping from head to foot, from every pore, with blood and dirt' (1976: 926).

He has some sardonic comments to make about 'the Christian character of primitive accumulation' and the 'sober exponents of Protestantism, the Puritans of New England', who put a price on the scalp of native American men. Slavery and the slave trade were very visible expressions of this brute force and were important elements of primitive accumulation. Thus Liverpool, Marx says, 'grew fat on the slave trade'. The city's wealth was also rooted in the cotton industry which rose rapidly in the last quarter of the eighteenth century, with its factories in Lancashire and its raw materials in the southern states of United States. While in English cotton mills it introduced 'child-slavery', in the United States it transformed, in Marx's words, 'the earlier, more or less patriarchal slavery, into a system of commercial exploitation'. Thus, he says, 'the veiled slavery of the wage-labourers in Europe needed the unqualified slavery pure of the New World as its pedestal' (1976: 925).

The dominant form of capital in these early European commercial empires of the sixteenth- to eighteenth centuries was merchant capital. It was largely driven by the need to appropriate wealth and raw materials and to monopolize trade. Methods of production under the rule of merchant capital were still in many respects pre-capitalist in form and the direct impact on the pre-capitalist modes of production of the societies it was plundering was limited, if mostly destructive. This changed with the transition first to manufacture and then to industrial forms of production. 'To-day', Marx argued, 'industrial supremacy brings with it commercial supremacy. In the period of manufacture it is the reverse: commercial supremacy produces industrial predominance' (1976: 918). Merchant capital, dependent on monopolistic restrictions in trade, was increasingly swept aside by international free trade. Pre-capitalist forms of production in Asia and Africa could hardly survive in the face of industrial production which was already by the middle of the nineteenth century transforming Britain, and some other parts of Western Europe and the United States, into societies of unprecedented wealth and power. The history of the social division of labour and the transformation of the labour process, especially through machinery, is crucial for any understanding of the industrial capitalism of the present (of Marx's present). It is to this other, convergent, history in the pages of *Capital* that we now turn.

INDUSTRIAL REVOLUTION

For Marx, the recent history of Britain had been characterized by a massive and still incomplete transformation between two periods – the period of manufacture and the period of 'modern industry' – amounting to what he sometimes called an 'industrial revolution'. This receives extended treatment in the first volume of *Capital* – in chapters 13 to 15.

Marx begins with a straightforward model. The labour process has three 'simple elements':

> (1) purposeful activity, that is work itself, (2) the objects on which that work is performed, and (3) the instruments of that work. (1976: 284)

The labour process in this essential form is, Marx says, 'common to all forms of society in which human beings live'. However, it develops and changes throughout history. Under capitalism it has one very distinctive feature: it is not only about producing use values – in other words, something useful to people – but also about producing exchange value, in other words, something that can be sold at a profit; and this is because the ultimate purpose of production under capitalism is the generation of surplus value. 'Our capitalist', Marx says, wants to produce 'a commodity greater in value than the sum of the values of the commodities used to produce it, namely the means of production and the labour-power he purchased with his good money on the open market' (1976: 293). The labour process is therefore also a valorization process.

Marx's account of primitive accumulation had indicated how free labour emerged out of a social and political history of dispossession, violence and legalized theft. His account of the transformation of the labour process similarly stresses questions of power and authority in appropriating resources out of the hands of the many and into the hands of the few. In early capitalism skilled artisans in workshops produced commodities for the market. Workshops were generally small – a master, a few journeymen and apprentices. Division of labour was restricted. The guilds were political and cultural representatives of this form of production. However, handicraft production and the power of the guilds were undermined as skilled craftsman increasingly lost control of the production process and small workshops were reorganized into bigger and more productive units. This kind of 'cooperation', based on the division of labour and the controlling will of a capitalist, assumes its classical shape according to Marx, in 'manufacture'. This is the characteristic form of production from around the middle of the sixteenth century to the last third of the eighteenth century (though of course it not only persists but successfully adapts to new conditions in the nineteenth century).

In its early phases, manufacture represents only a quantitative extension of simple co-operation. The technical instruments of production remained largely unchanged. Work is still performed by hand and it is therefore, Marx says, 'dependent on the strength, skill, quickness and sureness with which the individual worker manipulates his tools'. The skill of the craftsman remains the foundation of the production process. However, though the technical level of manufacturing remains rudimentary, increasing division of labour demands greater co-ordination of the various operations. This sometimes involved the bringing together of separate trades under one roof, co-ordinating them in the manufacture of a specific commodity. More significant in the longer term was the breaking down of work which had formerly been carried out by a single handicraft worker into a series of separate operations performed by specialized workers. In Adam Smith's classical account of the manufacture of pins in *The Wealth of Nations* (1776) this is celebrated as a triumph of rationality, massively increasing the productivity of labour. By subdividing the specific tasks required in the making of a pin, ten men could produce around 4,800 pins in a day. If each man had had to perform every task himself then, Smith suggests, they would struggle to produce as many as 20 pins between them.[6] For Marx this was a significant achievement, but he is alert to the consequences in terms of social power and the experience of the worker. Through centralization and co-ordination 'the productive power of social labour' is brought under the more direct control of capital, generating greater profits and thus the further accumulation of both capital and power. 'Division of labour within the workshop implies the undisputed authority of the capitalist over men, who are merely the members of a total mechanism which belongs to him' (1976: 476–7). For the worker, division of labour brought with it deskilling and specialization, which meant loss of control over his own labour. This new work regime is, Marx says, 'in form, purely despotic':

> [T]he co-operation of wage-labourers is entirely brought about by the capital that employs them. Their unification into one single productive body, and the establishment of a connection between their individual functions, lies outside their competence. These things are not their own act, but the act of the capital that brings them together and maintains them in that situation. Hence the interconnection between their various labours confronts them, in the realm of ideas, as a plan drawn up by the capitalist, and, in practice, as his authority, as the powerful will of a being outside them, who subjects their activity to his purpose. (1976: 449–50)

A new and much more revolutionary transformation was, however, already under way. 'Manufacture produced the machinery with which large-scale industry abolished the handicraft and manufacturing systems in the spheres of production it first seized hold of' (1976: 504). The introduction of machinery into specific stages of production was gradual and initially confined to textiles, but its impact was soon felt in other areas. Introduction of new technologies into one stage of production led to further technological innovation, first within a specific industry but then broadening out into every area of society, generating radically new forces and relations of production and a new kind of industrial capitalism. And so we reach the dazzling modernity of mid-Victorian Britain with its towering factory chimneys, its feats of modern engineering, its great steam-ships and railway trains:

> [T]he means of communication and transport handed down from the period of manufacture soon became unbearable fetters on large-scale industry, given the feverish velocity with which it produces, its enormous extent, its constant flinging of capital and labour from one sphere of production into another and its newly-created connections with the world market. Hence, quite apart from the immense transformation which took place in shipbuilding, the means of communication and transport gradually adapted themselves to the mode of production of large-scale industry by means of a system of river steamers, railways, ocean steamers and telegraphs. But the huge masses of iron that had now to be forged, welded, cut, bored and shaped required for their part machines of Cyclopean dimensions, which the machine-building trades of the period of manufacture were incapable of constructing. (1976: 506)

Marx was well aware that industrialization did not turn all labour into factory work, but in fact produced an increasingly complex social structure. He carefully studied the census of occupations and remarked on how ‘the extraordinary increase in the productivity of large-scale industry, accompanied as it is by both a more intensive and a more extensive exploitation of labour-power in all other spheres of production, permits a larger and larger part of the working-class to be employed unproductively’ (1976: 574). Some of the profits appropriated by a minority of capitalists found their way into expenditure and the creation of jobs in luxury industries of various kinds and in domestic service. This question of the relations between productive and unproductive labour, a distinction developed by Adam Smith, was explored in great detail in the unpublished *Theories of Surplus Value*. The bourgeoisie was originally very thrifty, Marx comments, but increasingly it is imitating its feudal forebears in its employment of retainers. The 1861 census of England and Wales revealed that while the total employment in factories was around 775,000, there were more than a million female domestic servants:

> What a convenient arrangement it is that makes a factory girl to sweat twelve hours in a factory, so that the factory proprietor,

> with a part of her unpaid labour, can take into his personal service her sister as maid, her brother as groom and her cousin as soldier or policeman! (1969: 201)

A further point about the increasing complexity of industrial capitalism: the process of industrialization occurred gradually and unevenly within a system of various forms of manufacturing and many of these not only persisted in Victorian Britain but were stimulated by mechanization in other parts of the economy. Older forms of domestic and handicraft production often benefited, at least in the short run, from the resulting surplus labour and falling wages. At the same time there was a massive growth in both old and new kinds of labour associated with transport.

TECHNOLOGY AND HISTORY

Is Marx putting forward a technological interpretation of historical change in this account of industrial revolution? There are those within the Marxist tradition who have argued that technical change is the primary determinant of social change. They argue that, when Marx says in the 1859 'Preface', 'The mode of production of material life conditions the general process of social, political and intellectual life', and when he goes on to say that it is 'the material productive forces of society' which destabilize the existing relations of production, what he is pointing to is the dynamic force of technology at the core of the production process. The forces of production, in other words, are tools and machines, sources of energy, the material instruments of production. New technology produces new forms of production, new kinds of work, new social relations within the workplace. These in turn unsettle existing social relations and existing values, attitudes, beliefs and ideas outside the workplace. There is much to be said for this kind of explanatory schema. On occasion Marx does voice this kind of argument about the primacy of technology. A famous passage from *The Poverty of Philosophy* of 1847 can be read as a fairly straightforward assertion of technological determinism:

> Social relations are closely bound up with productive forces. In acquiring new productive forces men change their mode of production; and in changing their mode of production, in changing

> the way of earning their living, they change all their social relations. The hand-mill gives you society with the feudal lord; the steam-mill society with the industrial capitalist. (MECW6: 165)

However, there are passages and arguments where Marx clearly subsumes technology within a more complex argument about the forces of production. These also include labour-power, the knowledges, skills and energies of the worker and the scientist. Labour is of such immense importance in *Capital* precisely because it is always a dynamic and transformative point of interaction between consciousness and the material world, between human beings and their natural environment. The distinctive character of human labour is exemplified by Marx in a comparison of the weaver and the spider, the architect and the honey bee:

> A spider conducts operations which resemble those of the weaver, and the bee would put many a human architect to shame by the construction of its honeycomb cells. But what distinguishes the worst architect from the best of bees is that the architect builds the cell in his mind before he constructs it in wax. At the end of every labour-process, a result emerges which had already been conceived by the worker at the beginning, hence already existed ideally. Man not only effects a change of form in the materials of nature; he also realizes his own purpose in those materials. (1976: 284)

In other words, labour, as an exclusively human *activity*, is characterized by purpose, by *intentionality*. Through the practices of labour an ideal project realizes itself materially or, at least, modifies material reality and brings into existence new forms of objectivity. Labour-power, Marx says, is 'the aggregate of those mental and physical capabilities existing in the physical form, the living personality, of a human being, capabilities which he sets in motion whenever he produces a use-value of any kind' (1976: 270). However simple the task, the capacity of this living personality to respond intelligently to circumstances is what differentiates human labour from that of a machine.

So, the forces of production include conscious human action. Far from being 'the first mover unmoved', technology is as much the *result* as the cause of economic and social change. But again, note that this relationship is historical. The forces of production change and so does the role of human labour within them. The skilled craftsman in the workshop, the specialist handworker in a large manufacturing enterprise, the machine minder in a modern cotton mill are three stages in the subordination of labour to the rule of capital. They mark also a progressive degradation in the experience of labour as creativity, independence and initiative are reduced – though they are never entirely removed. At the core of this long process of deterioration of work is the separation of mental and manual labour – and note how this succinct history of labour is at the same time a history of the relations and the forces of production:

> This process of separation starts in simple cooperation, where the capitalist represents to the individual workers the unity and the will of the whole body of social labour. It is developed in manufacture, which mutilates the worker, turning him into a fragment of himself. It is completed in large-scale industry, which makes science a potentiality for production which is distinct from labour and presses it into the service of capital. (1976: 482)

What was once the practical knowledge of the craftsman – the accuracy of his eye, the feeling in his fingers tips for his tools and his materials accumulated through years of experience – has been appropriated by management in the form of scientific understanding and technical expertise. Graphs, rules, timetables and scientific instruments replace rule of thumb and the creative intelligence of the individual labourer. For the worker these systems of machines in large-scale industry completed the despotic power of capital, reducing individual initiative and creativity to a bare minimum.

So for Marx, development of the forces of production was not driven by some kind of neutral or progressive technical logic. On the contrary, technological rationality was a means of facilitating the extraction of surplus value and was thus the material expression of the power of capital over labour. Scientific and technical knowledge and the gigantic natural forces which are brought into play in modern production, contribute to 'the power of the master' (1976: 549). The factory is, then, a kind of political institution.[7] Marx speaks of the 'barrack-like discipline' of the factory, 'the autocracy of capital' and the 'autocratic power' and 'despotism' of the employer.

> The overseer's book of penalties replaces the slave-driver's lash. All punishments naturally resolve themselves into fines and deductions from wages, and the law-giving talent of the factory Lycurgus so arranges matters that a violation of his laws is, if possible, more profitable to him than the keeping of them. (1976: 550)

Marx sometimes uses military metaphors for the hierarchies of the workplace – soldiers, non-commissioned officers and so on. But, as *Capital* insists, 'the power of the master' materialized in the workplace, was never uncontested. In Britain by the middle of the eighteenth century manufacturing was in the ascendant. Nevertheless, its transformation of the labour process, especially via the division of labour and deskilling was neither smooth nor complete. It occurred over many generations and was bitterly resisted by strikes, riots and various forms of political action. As Marx commented, 'capital is constantly compelled to wrestle with the insubordination of the worker . . . Hence the complaint that the workers lack discipline runs through the whole of the period of manufacture'. And he goes on to note that during this period, from the sixteenth- to the late eighteenth century in Britain, 'capital failed in its attempt to seize control of the whole disposable labour-time of the manufacturing workers'. Manufacture, in other words, 'was unable either to seize upon the production of society to its full extent, or to revolutionize that production to its very core' (1976: 490).

This resistance of workers was the stimulus for mechanization, which was designed and deployed with a single aim – the strengthening of capital's subjection of labour. 'In England, strikes have regularly given rise to the invention and application of new machines', Marx commented in *The Poverty of Philosophy*. 'Machines were, it may be said, the weapon employed by the capitalist to quell the revolt of specialized labour' (MECW6: 208f.). In the long chapter 15 of *Capital*, 'Machinery and Large-Scale Industry', Marx explores how machinery was used by employers to undercut the bargaining position of workers:

> It is the most powerful weapon for suppressing strikes, those periodic revolts of the working class against the autocracy of

> capital . . . It would be possible to write a whole history of the inventions made since 1830, for the sole purpose of providing capital with weapons against working-class revolt. (1976: 562–3)

The struggle within the workplace continued in large-scale industry. Chapter 10 of the first volume of *Capital*, 'The Working Day', is a detailed account of how the length of the working day is always the outcome of a contest between two distinct and mutually exclusive interests: 'in the history of capitalist production, the determination of what is a working-day, presents itself as the result of a struggle, a struggle between collective capital, *i.e.,* the class of capitalists, and collective labour, *i.e.,* the working-class' (1976: 344).

So, the final bitter historical irony in Marx's account is that working-class resistance played a crucial role in the development of new forms of industrial technology and organization, designed to maximize the production of relative surplus-value. And, a further historical irony, this alien power, this industrial behemoth, breathing smoke and flame, was itself the product of human labour. Not only was it physically made by workers, it was paid for out of the surplus value generated by other workers. In other words, the exploited, accumulated labour of previous generations of workers, becomes the tool of exploitation and immiseration of living labour. It is, Marx says, 'the rule of past labour over living labour, which constitutes the essence of capital'. Or, in a more Gothic version of the same point: 'Capital is dead labour, that, vampire-like, only lives by sucking living labour, and lives the more, the more labour it sucks' (1976: 342).

The detailed accounts in *Capital* of how in Britain hand production was increasingly being replaced by machine production was a history of technology, but it was also a history of the organization and reorganization of work, in which the division of labour played a decisive role. Most of all, however, it was a history of the antagonism of labour and capital. The dynamic of this history was not technology but the various forms of antagonism generated out of the process of production – whether in the workshop, the weaver's shed or the cotton mill and whether this antagonism took the form of trade union activity, strike action, walk-outs over wages and working conditions, machine-breaking and sabotage, or political activity.[8] There is an important formulation in the third volume of *Capital* which explores further this question of political power within the workplace (and its corollary, the question of the workplace within political power):

> The specific economic form in which unpaid surplus labour is pumped out of the direct producers determines the relationship of domination and servitude, as this grows directly out of production itself and reacts back on it in turn as a determinant. On this is based the entire configuration of the economic community arising from the actual relations of production, and hence also its specific political form. It is in each case the direct relationship of the owners of the conditions of production to the immediate producers – a relationship whose particular form corresponds always to a certain level of development of the type and manner of labour, and hence to its social productive power – in which we find the innermost secret, the hidden basis of the entire social edifice, and hence also the political form of the relationship of sovereignty and dependence, in short, the specific form of state in each case. (1981: 927)

Marx is pointing here again to the relations of 'domination and servitude', or 'sovereignty and dependence', which sustain the relations of production. In other words, the relations of production always have a political content – something which is central to the histories of primitive accumulation and of industrialization in the first volume of *Capital*. But having said this much, Marx in the very next sentence makes some important qualifications of the point, drawing our attention once again to the untidiness and incoherence of any actual history and calling for empirical research:

> This does not prevent the same economic base – the same in its major conditions – from displaying variations and gradations in its appearance, as the result of innumerable different empirical circumstances, natural conditions, racial relations, historical influences acting from outside, etc., and these can only be understood by analysing these empirically given conditions. (1981: 927–8)

So once more Marx does not provide a cut-and-dried answer in simple analytical terms. His argument is not the last word, a closing of doors, a conclusion. On the contrary these arguments about 'so-called primitive accumulation' and the transformation of the labour process are an opening of doors onto the dazzling richness and complexity of the concrete. He presents us not with a completed thought – a philosophy of history – but with a task: analysis of empirically given conditions, concrete analysis of concrete situations, present and past.

CHAPTER 5

THE POLITICS OF LABOUR

> *It is a matter of the utmost importance. What is at stake is the* abolition of torture *for 1 1/2 million people, not including the adult male working men!*
>
> *(MECW42: 383)*

THE INTERNATIONAL WORKING MEN'S ASSOCIATION

In the middle of his great theoretical labour of contesting the legitimacy of political economy, Marx became involved in the day-to-day work of the International Working Men's Association (IWMA). This body was founded in September 1864 in London at a crowded meeting of English trade unionists and political refugees from across Europe; old Owenites and Chartists, mixed with Irish nationalists, German Socialists, French Proudhonists and Blanquists, Italian nationalists and Polish patriots. Marx was involved from the start and became the chief theorist of the IWMA. He was a member of its founding committee and of the crucial subcommittee which drafted its rules and founding documents. He subsequently wrote most of its key documents and was a member of its General Council until 1872, when it moved to New York. He was also involved in much of the everyday business of the IWMA. According to Friedrich Lessner, a tailor and former member of the Communist League, Marx rarely missed a meeting of the Council of the International and was also one of those who regularly went to a local pub after the meeting to continue discussions over a few beers.[1] By September 1867 Marx was confident enough of his influence within the IWMA to assure Engels that 'in the next revolution, which is perhaps nearer than it appears, we (that is, you and I) will have this powerful engine in our hands . . .' (MECW42: 423–4). However, conscious that among the membership there was suspicion of middle-class professionals in a working-class organization, Marx refused the chairmanship in 1866 and he rarely attended its international congresses.

The IWMA was involved in major political issues of the day. It organized mass meetings in support of Lincoln and the Union during the American Civil War. It convened several public meetings in support of the cause of Poland and to expose Russian abuses in Europe. But above all the IWMA committed itself to providing aid for 'the workmen of all countries in their struggle against capital'. It campaigned for a shorter working week, for legal limitation of the working day to eight hours, for the restriction of child labour and for the development of education and training. It provided practical support for trade unions involved in strike action. During the wave of European strikes between 1864 and 1868, the IWMA supported the Leipzig compositors' strike, the tailors' strikes of 1866 and 1867 in London and Edinburgh, the strike of Paris bronze-workers, the strike in Geneva among the building trades and the Belgian miners' revolt of 1868, among others.[2]

Engels thought that Marx's time would be better spent completing *Capital*. But, for Marx, the IWMA created an opportunity, for the first time, to be actively engaged with some of the most organized sections of the working class in Britain and in other parts of Europe, not least Germany. As he explained to Engels, he had departed from his usual rule not to respond to invitations from political groups because the new organization had a foothold in the trade union movement and had real 'powers' mobilized in it. Active involvement in the day-to-day business of political activity, especially among European and American trade unionists, gave him a much deeper insight into the real world of labour and fed into his critique of political economy and his writing of *Capital*. At the same time, his years of patient research in the British Library, alongside his journalistic work, provided valuable ammunition in the political campaigns of the IWMA. For instance, in its 'Inaugural Address' Marx deployed his remarkable expertise, as formidable and impressive as any M.P. speaking in the House of Commons.

Here for example is part of his opening argument about the increasing inequalities of British society:

> The income and property tax returns laid before the House of Commons on July 20, 1864, teach us that the persons with yearly incomes valued by the tax gatherer of 50,000 pounds and upwards had, from April 5, 1862, to April 5, 1863, been joined by a dozen and one, their number having increased in that single year from 67 to 80. The same returns disclose the fact that about 3,000 persons divide among themselves a yearly income of about 25,000,000 pounds sterling, rather more than the total revenue doled out annually to the whole mass of the agricultural laborers of England and Wales. Open the census of 1861 and you will find that the number of male landed proprietors of England and Wales has decreased from 16,934 in 1851 to 15,066 in 1861, so that the concentration of land had grown in 10 years 11 per cent. (1974: 76)

Few trade unionists in 1864 could speak and write with such forensic authority.

There are other examples of how his years of research in the British Museum and his critical engagement with political economy were to become a political asset. For instance, chapter 15 of *Capital*, 'Machinery and Large-Scale Industry', explained how machinery was used by employers to undercut the bargaining position of workers. This provided the theoretical basis for a General Council resolution to the 1868 Brussels Congress of the IWMA. Marx initiated a discussion on the effects of machinery at a Council meeting in January 1868. After further debate the Council agreed to Marx's resolution:

> Resolved:
> that on the one side machinery has proved a most powerful instrument of despotism and extortion in the hands of the capitalist class; that on the other side the development of machinery creates the material conditions necessary for the superseding of the wages-system by a truly social system of production. (MECW21: 9)

This was moved at the Brussels Congress in September 1868, supported by the reading of extracts from *Capital*. The resolution was subsequently printed in *The Times* and in other newspapers in Britain, France, Germany, the United States and elsewhere.

TRADE UNIONS

The interplay between Marx's critique of political economy and his practical political experience in the IWMA during the 1860s is demonstrated by his thinking on two key political issues: the role of trade unions; and the intervention of the state in the sphere of production via the Factory Acts. The trade union was the most significant form of working-class organization. Marx was always aware of its shortcomings. 'The capitalist can live longer without the worker than the worker can without him', he pointed out in the *1844 Manuscripts*. Employers' organizations were routine and effective. Among the workers unions were difficult to maintain in the face of illegality and other difficulties. Thus, Marx comments: 'The capitalist always wins' (1975: 282). In the following year in *The Condition of the Working Class in England*, Engels devoted considerable space to the development of trade unions. He concluded that they were not able 'to secure for their members higher wages than those which they would in any case obtain as a result of free competition between capitalists for skilled men'. 'The history of these unions is a long series of defeats of the working men, interrupted by a few isolated victories', Engels commented (2009: 226). Nevertheless, large numbers of workmen consistently supported unions and Engels conceded that they could have positive effects: 'If the manufacturers did not have to face mass organized opposition from the workers, they would always increase their own profits by continually reducing wages.' More important, they were staging posts on the road of the working class to revolutionary politics. The frequency of strikes proves, Engels said, 'to what extent the social war has broken out all over England'. And he went on:

> These strikes, at first skirmishes, sometimes result in weighty struggles; they decide nothing, it is true, but they are the strongest proof that the decisive battle between bourgeoisie and proletariat is approaching. They are the military school of the working-men in which they prepare themselves for the great struggle which cannot be avoided . . . (2009: 232–3)

This remained the position of Marx and Engels on trade unions. In periods of economic growth unions could force wages up. But during periods of depression they were powerless to resist a fall. Political economy is right, Marx says in his Brussels lectures of December 1847, in its diagnosis of the effects of trade unions: 'In the long run they cannot withstand the laws of competition. These combinations bring about new machines, a new division of labour, removal from one place of production to another. In consequence of all this a reduction of wages' (MECW6: 437). But, Marx goes on, the value of trade unions is not to be measured only by their short-term effects on wages. They are to be valued not in the present – the relationship of capital and labour is not eternal – but in the light of a post-capitalist future: 'they are the means of uniting the working class, of preparing for the overthrow of the entire old society with its class contradictions'. Marx celebrates the uncompromising generosity of workers who out of their limited resources create organizations dedicated to this future:

> He who wants to beat his adversary will not discuss with him the costs of the war. And how far the workers are from such mean-spiritedness is proved to the economists by the very fact that the best-paid workers form the most combinations and that the workers spend all they can scrape from their wages on forming political and industrial associations and meeting (the costs) of this movement. (MECW6: 437)

Unions were represented in similar terms in the *Communist Manifesto*. Union success in protecting wage levels was always limited, but union activity had long-term political benefits. 'Now and then the workers are victorious, but only for a time. The real fruit of their battles lies, not in the immediate result, but in the ever expanding union of the workers' (2002: 229).

During the 1850s Marx continued to identify trade unions as a means through which workers developed a sense of their own class identity. Observing closely the wave of strikes in 1853 – 'symptoms of the civil war preparing in England' – he commented that trade union action was 'the indispensable means of holding up the spirit of the labouring classes, of combining them into one great association against the encroachments of the ruling class, and of preventing them from becoming apathetic, thoughtless, more or less well-fed instruments of production' (1971: 189). The inevitable onset of economic depression would soon produce cuts in wage levels, but the strikes and union campaigns of 1853 would not be wasted. They would soon be carried over into the political field, Marx thought.

Once Marx became involved in the IWMA the usefulness of trade union action became an urgent and very sensitive practical question. He was forced to rethink his position. 'A good old codger, an old Owenist', a carpenter called John Weston, Marx told Engels in May 1865, was propounding before a special meeting of the IWMA: first 'that a general rate in the rise of the rate of wages would be of no benefit to the workers'; and second, 'that the trades unions for that reason, etc., are *harmful*.' This was hardly likely to encourage the support of organized labour for the work of the IWMA. As Marx commented, if these two propositions were accepted, 'we should be in a terrible mess, both in respect of the trades unions here and the infection of strikes now prevailing on the Continent' (MECW42: 159). It fell to Marx to present a reply to Weston before the General Council of the IWMA. This was expanded into a pamphlet, entitled *Value, Prices and Profit*, where the facts of life in a capitalist labour market were reaffirmed:

> [D]espite all the ups and downs, and do what he may, the working man will, on an average, only receive the value of his labour, which resolves into the value of his labouring power, which is determined by the value of the necessaries required for its maintenance and reproduction, which value of necessaries finally is regulated by the quantity of labour wanted to produce them. (MECW20: 144)

In other words, as political economy had always argued, in a situation where there was 'surplus labour' wages will tend to stabilize around the level of basic subsistence.

But (and here some qualifications were added) by its very nature labour power is not a commodity like other commodities. Its value is formed, Marx says, by two elements: 'the one merely physical, the other historical or social'. The first element, the physical limit, is set by the price of the indispensable necessities which a labourer needs to buy to survive – food, clothing, shelter – and the number of hours which a labourer can work before exhaustion and physical deterioration set in. Even this physical element is elastic. Wages can fall below subsistence level for extended periods: 'A quick succession of unhealthy and short-lived generations will keep the labour market as well supplied as a series of vigorous and long-lived generations.' In other words, starving and overworking the workforce into premature death is not a problem for employers as long as there is a plentiful supply of labour to fill the gaps.

The second element, the social or historical, is where Marx introduced some cautious modifications into the argument – and distanced the IWMA from the kinds of arguments voiced by Weston. In different parts of Europe there were different assumptions about what constituted a fair day's work or reasonable accommodation or a minimum diet. According to Marx:

> [T]he value of labour is in every country determined by a *traditional standard of life*. It is not mere physical life, but it is the satisfaction of certain wants springing from the social conditions in which people are placed and reared up. The English standard of life may be reduced to the Irish standard; the standard of life of a German peasant to that of a Livonian peasant. (MECW20: 145)

These social and historical dimensions of wage levels are determined not by any economic law. They are the contingent outcomes of different histories and, ultimately, of the shifting balance of power between capital and labour:

> The fixation of its actual degree is only settled by the continuous struggle between capital and labour, the capitalist constantly tending to reduce wages to their physical minimum, and to extend the working day to its physical maximum, while the working man constantly presses in the opposite direction. The matter resolves itself into a question of the respective powers of the combatants. (MECW20: 146)

This grants a legitimate role for trade unions.

But Marx goes on to qualify any sense that unions, by industrial action alone, can significantly raise working-class living standards in the long run. To achieve this political action was required. The Factory Acts, which had begun to mark out clear limits to the working day, were a result of a concerted working-class political campaign: 'Without the working men's continuous pressure from without that interference would never have taken place.' This was not something that could have succeeded through localized union pressure exerted by workers on their employers. It came about through *political* pressure at a *national* level and through reform of the law in parliament. Marx is keen to emphasize here the limitations of union activity: 'This very necessity of *general political action* affords the proof that in its merely economical action capital is the stronger side' (MECW20: 146).

Towards the end of *Value, Price and Profit* Marx indicates the grim situation facing trade unions: 'the very development of modern industry must progressively turn the scale in favour of the capitalist against the working man, . . . the general tendency of capitalistic production is not to raise, but to sink the average standard of wages, or to push the *value of labour* more or less to its *minimum limit*.' Capital always holds the whip hand and can use various means, especially machinery, to engineer reductions in labour costs, that is, a fall in wages. This doesn't mean that unions should give up either 'making the best of the occasional chances for their temporary improvements' or resisting the constant downward pressure of capital on wages: 'By cowardly giving way in their everyday conflict with capital, they would certainly disqualify themselves for the initiating of any larger movement' (MECW20: 148). But in the end, the scope for effective action to raise wages is limited and he warns trade unionists of the danger of becoming entirely focused on the endless guerilla war against the encroachments of capital and fluctuations in the economy:

> They ought not to forget that they are fighting with effects, but not with the causes of those effects; that they are retarding the downward movement, but not changing its direction; that they are applying palliatives, not curing the malady. (MECW20: 148)

For Marx and Engels trade unions, at their worst, locked workers into an endless, wearying, localized struggle against inevitable defeat and deflected them from the only solution to excessive labour and low wages – not a fair day's wage for a fair day's work, but the abolition of the wages system through concerted *political* action. On the other hand, at their best, trade unions mitigated the worst effects of capitalism in the workplace and offered some protection. Most important, they provided the experience through which a much more coherent and politically self-conscious working class would develop. As Marx put it in an important document prepared for a congress of the IWMA in 1866, trade unions pointed to a future beyond capitalism. They were centres of organization for the working class in the same way as the medieval communes had been for the middle class. 'If the trade unions are required for the guerilla fights between capital and labour, they are still more important as *organised agencies for superseding the very system of wage labour and capital rule*' (1974: 91).[3] Trade unions, too narrowly focused on 'local and immediate struggles with capital', had not fully realized their historical mission to become 'the champions and representatives of the whole working class' and to serve as 'organizing centers of the working class in the broad interest of its complete emancipation' (1974: 91–2).

THE POLITICS OF THE FACTORY

As *Value, Prices and Profit* had indicated, the question of the Factory Acts was of immense political significance. Chapter 10 of the first volume of *Capital*, 'The Working Day', indicates how Marx's critique of political economy connected with day-to-day politics within the sphere of production and spoke directly to organized labour. Surplus value is what is produced in the time remaining after the amount of labour-time necessary for the worker to earn enough for the provision of his necessities is subtracted. The quantity of absolute surplus-value extracted thus varies according to the length of the working day. The total length of the working day is therefore a matter of immense importance to the capitalist. There are human limits to the working day, because labour-power is attached to a human body which requires food, rest, sleep, and so on. In its incessant drive to maximize absolute surplus-value, capital pushes against even these physical limits, allowing little time for the fulfilment of the most basic human needs.

Marx goes on to underline the way in which the individual worker is dehumanized, turned into a function within the production process – one which is, if necessary, expendable:

> [Capital] usurps the time for growth, development and healthy maintenance of the body. It steals the time required for the consumption of fresh air and sunlight. It haggles over the meal-times,

> where possible incorporating them into the production process itself, so that food is added to the worker as to a mere means of production, as coal is supplied to the boiler, and grease and oil to the machinery. It reduces the sound sleep needed for the restoration, renewal and refreshment of the vital forces to the exact amount of torpor essential to the revival of an absolutely exhausted organism. It is not the normal maintenance of labour-power which determines the limits of the working day here, but rather the greatest possible daily expenditure of labour-power, no matter how diseased, compulsory and painful it may be, which determines the limits of the workers' period of rest. Capital asks no questions about the length of life of labour-power. (1976: 375–6)

Any limit to the working day was for the capitalist a restriction on profit-making. His relation to the worker was not a relation to another human being but to a lucrative source of labour power and thus of surplus value. Capital achieves the extraction of the maximum of surplus value 'by shortening the life of labour-power, in the same way as a greedy farmer snatches more produce from the soil by robbing it of its fertility'. Extension of the working day, Marx says, 'not only produces a deterioration of human labour-power by robbing it of its normal moral and physical conditions of development and activity, but also produces the premature exhaustion and death of this labour-power itself'. The new factories pioneered this destruction of its workforce but their ruthless methods spread into other areas of production, including workshop trades and even domestic industry.

Using parliamentary commissions, the reports of the Factory Inspectors, as well as newspapers and other sources, *Capital* documented the brutal consequences of this 'vampire thirst for the living blood of labour', providing many individual case studies:

> From the motley crowd of labourers of all callings, ages and sexes, who throng around us more urgently than did the souls of the slain around Ulysses, on whom we see at a glance the signs of over-work, without referring to the Blue Books under their arms, let us select two more figures, whose striking contrast proves that before capital all men are alike – a milliner and a blacksmith. (1976: 364)

Marx goes on to document in detail the fate of a young milliner in London, whose death from over-work was reported in the London daily papers in June, 1863.

Mary Anne Walkley was 20 years of age when she died. She was one of 60 girls employed in the very respectable dress-making establishment of 'Madame Elise' on Regent Street in the West End of London. They often worked for 16 and a half hours at a stretch, but in the London season this increased to as much as 30 hours, stimulated by occasional doses of alcohol and coffee, in two crowded rooms lacking adequate ventilation. They slept in equally overcrowded and ill-ventilated bedrooms. 'It was the height of the season', Marx recounted. 'It was necessary, in the twinkling of an eye, to conjure up magnificent dresses for the noble ladies invited to the ball in honour of the newly imported Princess of Wales'. After working for 26 and a half hours without a break, Mary Anne Walkley was taken ill and died soon after – 'without, to the astonishment of Madame Elise, having finished off the bit of finery she was working on'. The doctor's opinion, before the coroner's jury, was that she had died from overwork in overcrowded conditions (1976: 364–5).[4]

This is just one of many case studies in *Capital* of the reality of over-work and the increased mortality that resulted. However, workers were never the passive victims of these processes of dehumanization. There is an active politics of resistance within the workplace. The length of the working day is always, Marx argues, 'the product of a protracted civil war, more or less dissembled, between the capitalist class and the working-class'. It was a struggle which revealed the inequalities at the heart of the 'contract' between labour and capital. The wage bargain, according to political economy, is free. It is a contract agreed to by free and equal parties – those selling and those buying a certain quantity of labour power. But, Marx emphasizes, there is a profound inequality between the two parties. The buyer of labour power has resources to spare for his own and his family's needs. The seller of labour power, on the other hand, has little or nothing and is therefore, in order to survive, compelled to sell the only thing of value which he or she has. The wage-labourer, Marx drily observes, 'freely' bargains himself, and sometimes his family, into 14, 16 or more hours of dirty, exhausting and life-threatening work and for a wage that often barely covers subsistence. What they find themselves compelled to do at work further demonstrates the imbalance of power between the parties:

> The contract by which he sold his labour-power to the capitalist proved in black and white, so to speak, that he was free to dispose of himself. But when the transaction was concluded, it was discovered that he was no 'free agent', that the period of time for which he is free to sell his labour-power is the period of time for which he is forced to sell it, that in fact the vampire will not let go 'while there remains a single muscle, sinew or drop of blood to be exploited'. (1976: 415–16)

In order to set limits to their own self-exploitation, as Marx ironically puts it, the labourers campaigned successfully for the introduction of legislation which will provide, 'an all-powerful social barrier by which they can be prevented from selling themselves and their families into slavery and death by voluntary contract with capital'. And Marx cannot resist a final sarcastic gibe about how the Factory Acts replaced 'the pompous catalogue of the "inalienable rights of man"' with 'the modest Magna Charta of a legally limited working-day' (1976: 416). Note that in English political thinking Magna Carta was one of the great originary moments in the development of civil liberty. It established, at least in principle, that kings were bound by the rule of law in their treatment of their subjects.[5]

The successful passage into law of the Ten Hours Act of 1846, was not just a political victory with practical benefits for working people. It was also, Marx said in the Inaugural Address of the IWMA, an immense victory in the intellectual struggle between competing versions of political economy, 'between the blind rule of the supply and demand laws which form the political economy of the middle class, and social production controlled by social foresight, which forms the political economy of the working class . . . it was the victory of a principle; it was the first time that in broad daylight the political economy of the middle class succumbed to the political economy of the working class' (1974: 79). However, it was merely a battle won in a war that was far from over. The Factory Acts, by establishing a normal working day in terms of hours of labour, pushed capitalists towards other ways of increasing the quantity of surplus value extracted from labour. It tended to sweep away small firms in favour of larger ones, it increased the concentration of capital and it accelerated the transformation of the labour process. Part Four of Capital, 'The Production of Relative Surplus-Value', investigated how relative surplus-value is produced through the increased intensity, and thus increased productivity, of labour. This requires both a more efficient organization of labour and the further development of the means of production, especially through the application of technology. This new machine technology, as we have seen Marx stress at several points in *Capital*, was designed and deployed with a single aim – the strengthening of capital's subjection of labour in order to maximize the extraction of relative surplus-value.

So among the effects of the Factory Acts was an intensification of labour for many workers. Some of the most passionate invectives in *Capital* are directed against the use of machinery in the factory. It is, Marx says, an infernal creature – 'a mechanical monster whose body fills entire factories, and whose demonic power, at first hidden by the slow and measured motions of its gigantic members, finally bursts forth in the fast and feverish whirl of its countless working organs' (1976: 503). In this inferno, the workers are reduced to a mere means of production, slaves of the machine. 'In handicrafts and manufacture, the worker makes use of a tool; in the factory, the machine makes use of him' (1976: 548). The system of machinery in the factory, Marx says, is 'a lifeless mechanism independent of the workman, who becomes its mere living appendage'. Thus labour is further degraded, transformed from intelligent and creative activity into a form of physical suffering:

> Factory work exhausts the nervous system to the uttermost; at the same time it does away with the many-sided play of the muscles, and confiscates every atom of freedom, both in bodily and in intellectual activity. Even the lightening of the labour becomes an instrument of torture since the machine does not free the worker from the work, but rather deprives the work itself of all content. (1976: 548)

'Every sense organ is injured', Marx says, by the heat, the dust and the deafening noise. The experience of labour was little more than an extended physical torture, distorting the body and the mind.

This was not a result of machinery per se but of its ruthless application by employers, with a number of paradoxical effects.

Machinery which could reduce the necessary the hours of labour had in practice increased them; machinery which could lighten labour had in practice made it harder; machinery which in itself is, Marx says, 'a victory of man over the forces of nature', had in practice made men slaves of those forces; and machinery which increased the production of wealth had reduced those who produced it to poverty. The Factory Acts were not the ultimate solution to the problem of human brutalization in factories and workplaces. But they did mitigate some of its worst examples. And they moved the struggle of labour forward, providing an important political space both to contest the power of capital and to generate further working-class activity and organization.

As he was drafting and redrafting chapter 10 of *Capital*, Marx kept a sharp eye not just on new Factory Inspector's reports but on the minutiae of parliamentary business. Thus a footnote to an account of the extension of legislation to protect labouring children in a new range of industries notes: 'Since 1866, when I wrote the above passage, a reaction has set in once again.' Sending another draft section of *Capital* to Engels, in June 1867, Marx reported that some employers were now calling for a new enquiry into the employment of children; 'a fresh sample of what swine they are', Marx growled. This was, he accused, a cynical strategy to engineer 'a new 5-year lease for exploitation' by delaying implementation of legal restrictions set out by the Children's Employment Commission:

> Fortunately, my position in the 'International' enables me to frustrate those curs' little game. It is a matter of the utmost importance. What is at stake is the *abolition of torture* for 1 1/2 million people, not including the adult male working men! (MECW42: 383)

Marx encouraged action by the union leaders in the General Council to oppose any relaxing of the already weak laws protecting working children. The scheming of employers was, in this instance, defeated and in August 1867 Parliament did limit the working day for women and children under 18 to ten and a half hours, not only in large factories but in small enterprises and in domestic industry.

Here again we can see the interplay between theoretical critique of political economy and immediate political practice. A brief statement on the effects of machinery at a meeting of the General Council in July 1868 further demonstrates how complex theoretical arguments in *Capital* about the shift from absolute to relative surplus value had direct political implications. The increased use of machinery and of a more complex and efficient kind has increased the intensity of labour so that, Marx says, more work is now done in the short day than in the long day before any Factory Acts were introduced. As a result: 'People are again overworked, and it will soon become necessary to limit the working day to eight hours.' The use of machinery increases the power of capital over labour in various ways. The labour of women and children can be exploited, sources of labour-power more amenable to discipline than adult men. At the same time, the reduction in the demand for skilled labour generates a surplus in the labour market, again making labour more tractable and pulling wages down.

> The factory lord has become a penal legislator within his own establishment, inflicting fines at will, frequently for his own aggrandisement. The feudal baron in his dealings with his serfs was bound by traditions and subject to certain definite rules; the factory lord is subject to no controlling agency of any kind. (MECW21: 382)

The Magna Charta of the Factory Acts was as limited as its thirteenth-century original and marked merely a first uncertain step towards civil liberty and the rule of law inside the workplace.

A final point about the Factory Acts: Marx was immensely impressed by the publications generated by the British state around these questions and the impartial role of the various professionals involved As he commented to his German readers in the preface to the first edition of *Capital*:

> We should be appalled at our own circumstances if, as in England, our governments and parliaments periodically appointed commissions of inquiry into economic conditions; if these commissions were armed with the same plenary powers to get at the truth; if it were possible to find for this purpose men as competent, as free from partisanship and respect of persons as are England's factory inspectors, her medical reporters on public health, her commissioners of inquiry into the exploitation of women and

> children, into conditions of housing and nourishment, and so on. (1976: 91)

Some of the most powerful writing in *Capital* was drawn from the reports of the Children's Employment Commission and its details of the appalling working conditions of many children.

THE RESERVE ARMY OF LABOUR

The workplace was one dimension of the oppression of the worker. Another, its antithesis, was the noisy 'sphere of circulation', where the sale and purchase of labour-power went on. The dynamic relation between what goes on in the sphere of production and what goes on in the wider society (the sphere of circulation) is represented by Marx in *Capital* in an antithesis – 'anarchy in the social division of labour and despotism in the manufacturing division of labour'. The latter is characterized by 'a concentration of the means of production in the hands of one capitalist' and the 'complete subjection' of the worker to the undisputed authority of the capitalist. But in the wider society anarchy takes the form of a 'necessity imposed by nature, controlling the unregulated caprice of the producers, and perceptible in the fluctuations of the barometer of market prices'. Labour thus experiences two forms of social authority – the despotism of the workplace and the arbitrary authority of competition imposed through the coercive laws of the market (1976: 476–7).

It was in the sphere of circulation – 'within whose boundaries the sale and purchase of labour-power goes on' – that many working people found themselves stranded, impoverished and unemployed. Marx described it as 'this noisy sphere, where everything takes place on the surface and in full view of everyone' and expands into a brilliant sarcastic peroration on the public world of the free market, this 'very Eden of the innate rights of man':

> It is the exclusive realm of Freedom, Equality, Property and Bentham. Freedom, because both buyer and seller of a commodity, let us say of labour-power, are determined only by their own free will. They contract as free persons, who are equal before the law. Their contract is the final result in which their joint will finds a common legal expression. Equality, because each enters into relation with the other, as with a simple owner of commodities, and

> they exchange equivalent for equivalent. Property, because each disposes only of what is his own. And Bentham, because each looks only to his own advantage. The only force bringing them together, and putting them into relation with each other, is the selfishness, the gain and the private interest of each. Each pays heed to himself only, and no one worries about the others. And precisely for that reason, either in accordance with the pre-established harmony of things, or under the auspices of an omniscient providence, they all work together to their mutual advantage, for the common weal and in the common interest. (1976: 280)

The reality of the free market for the seller of labour-power was somewhat different. And to investigate this question Marx developed the concept of 'reserve army of labour'.

In *The Condition of the Working Class in England* in 1845 Engels had already noted the existence, and the value to employers, of 'an unemployed reserve army of workers':

> This reserve army . . . is the 'surplus population' of England, which keeps body and soul together by begging, stealing, street-sweeping, collecting manure, pushing hand-carts, driving donkeys, peddling, or performing occasional small jobs. In every great town a multitude of such people may be found. It is astonishing in what devices this 'surplus population' takes refuge. (2009: 119)

Engels is evidently unhappy about the term 'surplus population' and the whole Malthusian explanation of poverty which was so influential in shaping social policy towards the poor at this time.[6] This branch of political economy was also the target of Marx's criticism.[7] In lectures in Brussels in 1847 he argued against the Malthusians, that what was called 'over-population' was not the result of the natural growth of population outstripping the means of subsistence. In a section titled, 'Competition among the Workers Themselves', Marx pointed to the role of unemployed and migrant labour in the fixing of wage levels: 'The wages of 1,000 workers of the same skill are determined not by the 950 in employment but by the 50 unemployed' (MECW6: 424). 'Big industry constantly requires a reserve army of unemployed workers . . .'. For Marx, far from being an effect of the laws of nature, declining wages, poverty and vagrancy were the outcomes of complex forces driving the accumulation of capital and revolutionizing the means of production (MECW 6: 432). Capitalists, Marx says in *Wage Labour and Capital*, published in 1849, 'vie with one another as to who can discharge the greatest number of industrial soldiers' (MECW9: 226). Those who remained in employment were working harder and longer in a desperate attempt to resist falling wage-rates. So, in an increasingly competitive labour market, wages fall and more and more workers find themselves out of work. At the same time, expansion on an ever-increasing scale increases the instability of the whole system and 'the industrial earthquakes' which, Marx says 'become more frequent and more violent'. These crises in turn exacerbate falling wages, unemployment and the economic insecurity of workers.

As his work was redirected to the central question of capitalist crisis in the 1850s, Marx developed a more complex understanding of the role of 'the reserve army of labour'. In *Capital* the 'reserve army' is divided into three rough strata: the floating, the latent and the stagnant. The first group, 'the floating', fluctuates in numbers and membership. It consists of those who are temporarily unemployed during periods of economic crisis and who find work when trade revives. The second group, 'the latent', consists of those not yet fully integrated into capitalist production – for example, parts of the rural population, or women performing unpaid household labour. 'The latent' thus forms a reservoir of potential labour which feeds into the floating stratum of the 'reserve army'. In boom periods some of 'the latent' reserve army are absorbed directly into employment. The third group, 'the stagnant', is more miscellaneous. It includes workers in 'domestic industry', what later became known as the sweated trades, characterized, Marx says, by 'extremely irregular employment'. 'Its conditions of life sink below the average normal level of the working-class; this makes it at once the broad basis of special branches of capitalist exploitation. It is characterised by maximum of working-time, and minimum of wages' (1976: 797). Then, finally, at the base of the 'stagnant' stratum is the 'lowest sediment' of the working class. These inhabit 'the sphere of pauperism' and are no longer strictly speaking an effective part of the reserve army:

> [T]he demoralised and ragged, and those unable to work, chiefly people who succumb to their incapacity for adaptation, due to

> the division of labour; people who have passed the normal age of the labourer; the victims of industry, whose number increases with the increase of dangerous machinery, of mines, chemical works, &c., the mutilated, the sickly, the widows, &c. Pauperism is the hospital of the active labour-army and the dead weight of the industrial reserve army. (1976: 797)

For Marx, the reserve army is crucial to the reproduction of capitalism. It is, he says, 'a lever of capitalistic accumulation, nay, a condition of existence of the capitalist mode of production'. It is the expansion and contraction of the reserve army that restrains wages and disciplines labour: 'The industrial reserve army, during the periods of stagnation and average prosperity, weighs down the active labour-army; during the periods of over-production and paroxysm, it holds its pretensions in check' (1976: 792). So whatever the economic conditions, the reserve army of labour undermines the bargaining power of those who are in work and whose job is never secure when there are others ready to replace him, or her. And, following on from this, it enables the working day and the intensity of labour to be extended beyond human limits by providing a source of potential workers to replace those prematurely destroyed by inhuman working conditions. 'Capital asks no questions about the length of life of labour-power' (1976: 375–6).

There is a moment when Marx seems close to underwriting the notion of 'surplus population' when he is discussing the stagnant stratum (or strata) of the reserve army of labour. These are by definition pretty much locked into their position in the labour market. And he notes their tendency towards larger families so that this pool of surplus labour is 'a self-reproducing and self-perpetuating element of the working-class'. But this is just one element of the 'lowest sediment' of the reserve army. The crucial point about the reserve army of labour is that it is not some kind of stable 'residuum' or 'underclass' made up of particular types of people. It is, on the contrary, a volatile and continuously reproduced presence within the labour market. Most workers – skilled as well as unskilled – experienced spells of unemployment and short-time working, many experienced migration and large numbers found themselves falling into the stagnant stratum of the reserve army at some point in their lives.

Mechanization was one process which brought this about, reducing the number of jobs in a particular industry as the organic composition of capital changed. As Marx puts it: 'The working population therefore produces both the accumulation of capital and the means by which it is itself made relatively superfluous; and it does this to an extent which it is always increasing' (1976: 783). But the reserve army was not just a product of mechanization. It was stressed again and again in the pages of *Capital* that modern forms of production were constantly transforming not only the technical basis of production but also the division of labour, moving capital rapidly from one branch of production to another and requiring the mobility of labour not just between different kinds of work but also across geographical space. Constant restructuring of production means a constant transformation of parts of the labouring population into migrant workers, casual labour or the unemployed. This, he says, 'does away with all repose, all fixity and all security as far as the worker's life situation is concerned' and 'constantly threatens . . . to snatch from his hands the means of subsistence' (1976: 617–18). In another section of the first volume of *Capital*, 'The Nomad Population', Marx underlines the contingency and fluidity of the reserve army as a social category. These 'nomads' are workers, generally drawn from the rural population, who are employed in short-term projects – as navvies on the railways, for instance, or as building workers or brickmakers. 'They are the light infantry of capital, thrown by it, according to its needs, now to this point, now to that. When they are not on the march, they "camp"' (1976: 818).

Here is one example of how the dynamic between the spheres of production and circulation (the labour market) worked itself out on the streets of London. Many children, Marx says, 'are from their earliest years riveted to the most simple manipulations, and exploited for years, without being taught a single kind of skill that would afterwards make them of use, even in the same factory' (1976: 615). He gives a particular example, drawn from what he describes as the 'thoroughly conscientious investigations of the Children's Employment Commission'. Formerly, apprentices in the letterpress printing trade had been taken through a course of training requiring the ability to read and write so that, after a period of several years, they became skilled printers. The introduction of the printing machine destroyed this work-culture. Now boys from the age of 11 were employed in two very simple mechanical tasks, repeated for up to 16 hours at a stretch. At 17 most were discharged, illiterate, lacking any skills and unfitted for other kinds of work. 'They become recruits for crime', Marx commented. Thrown onto the streets, whatever their individual biographies, these displaced and unskilled lads were not merely 'surplus population': they were products of the restructuring of production and the labour market to fit the requirements of capital. A social history of the surplus population would have to include many such narratives of the interaction between the transformation of the labour process and the labour market.

CONCLUSION

Marx emphasizes the discrepancy between the noisy sphere of circulation on the one hand – this 'very Eden of the innate rights of man' – and, on the other, the silence of the sphere of production, where men and women as well as children were enslaved and compelled to work themselves into an early grave. This is why he was often impatient with the political language of rights. It was a language which applied only as far as the factory door. Behind it the employer was an absolutist despot. Here there was no freedom of speech, no rights of the individual, no liberty of conscience. Marx grumbled to Engels about being forced to insert a couple of phrases about duty, right, truth, morality and justice into the Preamble to the Rules of the IWMA. Elsewhere in his writings after 1848 there are hostile comments about this kind of language. In the *Critique of the Gotha Programme* he denounced the 'ideological nonsense about right and other trash so common among the democrats and French socialists'. And in a letter in October 1877 he complained about the replacement of the materialist basis of socialism by 'modern mythology with its goddesses of Justice, Liberty, Equality and Fraternity', among some of the newer sections of SPD membership, mostly 'half-mature students and super-wise Doctors of Philosophy' (1975b: 290).

Many commentators have been quick to comment on the lack of a developed theory of politics and the state in the later Marx, thus by-passing the political content of *Capital.* Marx's concentration on political economy was precisely because it opened a way into the hidden sphere of production which was, he believed, the inner structure of the whole social order. A critique of political economy thus had immediate political implications by exposing a reality which the language of contracts, free labour and so on mystifies and conceals. This marked out Marx's political task: to combat vulgar political economy. 'I hope to win a scientific victory for our party', he told one of his correspondents on the eve of the publication of his *Contribution to a Critique of Political Economy* in 1859 (MECW40: 374). *Capital* was intended to contribute to practical political work. When the first French translation began to appear in instalments in the early 1870s, Marx was enthusiastic. To make the book more accessible to the working class was, he commented in the preface, 'a consideration which to me outweighs everything else'. But he went on to qualify this. He forewarned readers, eager to get from general principles to 'the immediate questions that have aroused their passions', that his method of dealing with economic subjects in the opening chapters was new and difficult: 'There is no royal road to science, and only those who do not dread the fatiguing climb of its steep paths have a chance of gaining its luminous summits' (1976: 104). Marx's battle against political economy was not some kind of cerebral exercise. It was connected to contemporary political debates and contemporary political antagonisms. For Marx, there were not one but two class-based 'political economies' locked in an extended political confrontation in Britain between the 1830s and the 1860s.

Nevertheless, whatever his bitter scepticism about the political force of this language of 'the innate rights of man', it clearly did contribute to radical working-class movements such as Chartism in Britain in the 1840s. And, as in the case of the Factory Acts, it contributed to the real (if limited) improvement of the working lives of hundreds of thousands of men, women and children. Marx's contrast between 'the pompous catalogue of the "inalienable rights of man"' and the real achievement of the Factory Acts which he calls 'the modest Magna Charta of a legally limited working-day', conceded this point (1976: 416). Political practice in the noisy public sphere of circulation remained the basis of any future 'emancipation' – a term from contemporary campaigns against slavery and the slave trade that Marx and Engels used time and again. Marx's farewell address 'To the Workers of Cologne', on behalf of the editors of the *Neue Rheinische Zeitung*, in May 1849, stated: 'their last word everywhere and always will be: *emancipation of the working class*' (MECW9: 467). And the 'Rules and Administrative Regulations of the International Workingmen's Association', drafted by Marx in

1867, stated: 'the emancipation of the working classes means not a struggle for class privileges and monopolies, but for equal rights and duties, and the abolition of all class rule' (MECW20: 441). The issue of a socialist politics, especially in the 1870s, is the focus of the next chapter.

CHAPTER 6

REFORM AND REVOLUTION

> *In presence of an unbridled reaction which violently crushes every effort at emancipation on the part of the working men . . .*
>
> *Considering that against this collective power of the propertied classes the working class cannot act, as a class, except by constituting itself as a political party, distinct from, and opposed to, all old parties formed by the propertied classes;*
>
> *That this constitution of the working class into a political party is indispensable in order to ensure the triumph of the social revolution and its ultimate end – the abolition of classes;*
>
> *That the combination of forces which the working class has already effected by its economical struggles ought at the same time to serve as a lever for its struggles against the political power of landlords and capitalists –*
>
> *The Conference recalls to the members of the International:*
>
> *That in the militant state of the working class, its economical movement and its political action are indissolubly united.*
>
> *(1974: 270)*

In the 1859 Preface to the *Critique of Political Economy* Marx had sketched out a plan of work which included six 'books': Capital, Landed Property, Wage Labour, the State, Foreign Trade, World Market. Marx focused his attention in the 1860s on capital, land and labour, though the first volume of *Capital* had included extended investigations of state intervention in the sphere of production, especially around the Factory Acts. It had also probed the limits of dominant discourses, politicizing the sphere of production by demonstrating the power structures that shaped the relations of capital and labour. *Capital* – as previous chapters have argued – was a profoundly political book. However, Marx's projected book on the state remained unwritten. In the years after the publication of *Capital* Marx was forced to deal with the political realities of the new expansive phase of capitalism in Western Europe. The Paris Commune of 1871 and the emergence of a mass socialist party in Germany in 1875 raised new questions about political strategy, about the tensions between reform and revolution, about the relations between parties and intellectual leadership and programmes on the one hand and the working class on the other. In these years Marx drafted a number of important works which contained elements of a theory of the state and of the politics of the transition from capitalism to communism: *The Civil War in France* (1870–1), his notes on Bakunin's book *State and Anarchy* (1874) and the *Critique of the Gotha Programme* (1875).

INTELLECTUALS AND POLITICS

Marx and Engels had always been clear that it was not the role of the political intellectual to set out blueprints for socialism. As *The German Ideology* succinctly put it, communism is not an ideal which will be imposed on reality: 'We call communism the *real* movement which abolishes the present state of things.' *The Communist Manifesto* had voiced Marx's derision of utopian schemers: 'the theoretical conclusions of the Communists are in no way based on ideas or principles that have been invented, or discovered, by this or that would-be universal reformer'. On the contrary, the principles and the practices of Communists merely 'express, in general terms, actual relations springing from an existing class struggle, from a historical movement going on under our very eyes' (2002: 234–5). Monitoring the political situation in Paris in the summer of 1850, Engels noted that among even the most politicized sections of the working class of Paris there was indifference towards the old socialist programmes and a deep distrust of all their recent political leaders, even Blanqui. He found grounds for optimism in this.

> The people, once thinking for themselves, freed from the old socialist tradition, will soon find socialist and revolutionary formulas which shall express their wants and interests far more

> clearly than anything invented *for them,* by authors of systems and by declaiming leaders. (MECW10: 35)

Once having achieved this kind of independence and maturity, he went on, 'the people will again be enabled to avail themselves of whatever talent and courage may be found among the old leaders, without becoming the tail of any of them'.

Marx remained suspicious of political intellectuals and utopian reformers and retained a degree of optimism about the capacity of working-class people to find their way to an uncompromising revolutionary position. In a speech on the seventh anniversary of the IWMA in 1871, Marx stated that its foundation was not the work of 'any set of clever politicians': 'What was new in the International was that it was established by the working men themselves and for themselves' (1974: 271). Its programme, he went on, is limited to some general points, 'leaving the details of theory to be worked out as inspired by the demands of the practical struggle, and as growing out of the exchange of ideas among the sections, with an equal hearing given to all socialist views in their journals and congresses' (1974: 299). A single example: in one of his instructions for the delegates to the Geneva Congress in 1866, on the question of co-operatives, Marx said that it was not their business to issue specific and top-down directives on how these should be organized. The IWMA's purpose was, he went on, 'to combine and generalize the *spontaneous movements* of the working classes, but not to dictate or impose any doctrinary system whatever' (1974: 90).

This was in part a tactical recognition of political realities. It was not practical to think in terms of exporting a set of political ideas and practices from one country to another, even within the limited geographical space of Western Europe. 'Since the sections of the working class in various countries have reached different stages of development, it follows that their theoretical opinions, which reflect the real movement, will be equally divergent,' Marx stated in an official circular in 1869. It is no part of the functions of the General Council, he said, to adjudicate on what was or was not 'a genuine expression of the proletarian movement'. As long as there was broad agreement on what he termed 'our Association's general tendency', then each section was 'free to formulate its own theoretical programme'. Having said that, 'the community of action' which they had established, their exchange of ideas through various publications and their face-to-face discussions at the IWMA's regular congresses would, in the long run, lead to agreement among all sections and 'a common theoretical programme' (1974: 280–1). It was a mistake to think of the IWMA as some kind of centralized and controlling organization, Marx told an American journalist in 1871. It was, he said, 'a bond of union rather than a controlling force'. It did not dictate policy to its network of affiliated societies but supported 'local energy and independence':

> In each part of the world some special aspect of the problem presents itself, and the workmen there address themselves to its consideration in their own way . . . The choice of that solution is the affair of the working classes of that country. The International does not presume to dictate in the matter and hardly to advise. (1974: 394–5)

More was at stake here than a pragmatic stance towards the wide differences in political experience and history of the labour movements in different parts of Europe. As a matter of principle there could never be any single and a priori political strategy – and especially not one worked out by intellectuals detached from the concrete problems and real situation of a working-class political movement. This featured in Marx's response to two major political events of the 1870s: the Paris Commune and the formation in 1875 of the first mass socialist party in Europe – the German Social Democrats.

In France in March 1871, at the end of a disastrous war with Germany and a humiliating peace, there was a popular uprising and a new revolutionary regime was installed in Paris. The red flag – 'symbol of the republic of labour', according to Marx – fluttered over the Hotel de Ville. Short-lived Communes were also set up in Lyons, Marseilles and other cities. The Paris Commune set about creating a new kind of popular government. There were hundreds of new initiatives. Committees, co-operatives, women's groups, free schools proliferated. Anarchists, Socialists, Communists, trade unionists co-operated, argued, disputed. The Commune lasted barely ten weeks before government troops penetrated the city. After a week or so of bloody street fighting the Commune was destroyed. According to a conservative historian of France 30,000 were killed in the fighting, perhaps as many as 50,000 later executed or imprisoned and 7,000 were exiled to a Pacific prison island.[1] In each of these categories there were members of the IWMA. Marx engaged in intense efforts to co-ordinate international support for the Paris Commune. Within a few weeks of its brutal suppression he had drafted a passionate defence of the Commune on behalf of the IWMA: *The Civil War in France: Address of the General Council.* This brought him some public notoriety as 'the Red Terror Doctor', mastermind of the omnipotent International which had engineered the Paris uprising.

For Marx the significance of the Commune was that it was initiated by working-class people themselves as a practical solution to a crisis situation: 'It was essentially a working-class government, the product of the struggle of the producing class against the appropriating class, the political form at last discovered under which to work out the economic emancipation of labour' (1974: 212). To this end, the Commune initiated new forms of political organization. The 92 members of the 'Communal Council' were elected, not as representatives but as delegates, in principle subject to recall by their electors at any time. In this way the Commune did away with the professional politicians – what he called 'the state parasite' – with distinct interests of their own to pursue. 'Instead of deciding once in three or six years which member of the ruling class was to misrepresent the people in Parliament, universal suffrage was to serve the people, constituted in Communes . . .', Marx commented (MECW22: 332). He was equally impressed by the decentralization of political power. 'Public functions ceased to be the vital property of the tools of the central government. Not only municipal administration, but the whole initiative hitherto exercised by the state was laid into the hands of the Commune' (1974: 209). In the draft plan of the Paris Communards, centralized government was replaced by a system of interlocking, self-governing communes, each electing its own assemblies to administer its own affairs. This pointed forward, Marx thought, to 'the self-government of the producers' (1974: 210, 252, 267).

The Commune was, for Marx, not a revolution against this or that government, or even this or that form of the state: 'It was a revolution against the state itself, this supernaturalist abortion of society, a resumption by the people for the people of its own social life' (1974: 249). It was, he said, 'a revolution to break down this horrid machinery of class domination itself'. The Communards were engaged in the 'reabsorption of the State power by society'. For Marx (and Engels) the Paris Commune was a heroic prefiguring of a post-capitalist society:

> The working class did not expect miracles from the Commune. They have no ready-made utopias to introduce *par decret du peuple*. They know that in order to work out their own emancipation, and along with it that higher form to which present society is irresistibly tending by its own economical agencies, they will have to pass through long struggles, through a series of historic processes, transforming circumstances and men. They have no ideals to realize, but to set free the elements of the new society with which old collapsing bourgeois society itself is pregnant. (1974: 213)

Once again the decisive point was that political innovation came not 'from above', via intellectuals and political cliques, but 'from below' – from the experience of the working class and their responses to real processes of change in the structures of economic and social life.

1875: *CRITIQUE OF THE GOTHA PROGRAMME*

The policies of the German SPD in the 1870s pointed in the opposite direction and provoked the writing of what is taken to be Marx's last general statement on political strategy. Marx's star was rising in Germany by this time. The *Communist Manifesto* was rediscovered through a new edition published in Germany in 1872. The first volume of *Capital* was brought out in a second edition in Germany in the same year. With the formation of the SPD, there now existed a mass socialist party which claimed some kind of affiliation to his ideas. However, the draft programme of the new Social-Democratic Workers' Party of Germany, formed of two major socialist groupings in 1875, provoked Marx to draft a sharp and critical response. Neither he nor Engels had been consulted about the drafting of this programme. They saw it for the first time in the newspapers. Engels responded quickly with a long and very critical letter (1975b: 290–5). A few weeks later Marx sent what he called his 'critical marginal notes on the Unity Programme' to some leading figures in the party. He threatened to publish a short statement disowning the whole programme: 'it is my duty not to give recognition, even by diplomatic silence, to what in my opinion is a thoroughly objectionable programme that demoralises the Party' (1975b: 278). Though the programme was approved by the Gotha congress, with a few minor changes, Marx and Engels chose to maintain silence. As Engels explained in a letter to Bebel a few months later, everyone seemed to be interpreting the Gotha Programme 'communistically': 'So long as our opponents as well as the workers continue to read our views into that programme, we are justified in saying nothing about it' (1975b: 280). Marx's critical notes were only published in 1891, as an intervention by Engels in further debates within the SPD.[2]

What were the main points of Marx's criticism? Four can be identified. First, the programme included this fatuous sectarian remark: 'The emancipation of labour must be the work of the working class, relative to which all other classes are only one reactionary mass.' It is political suicide, Marx says, to pronounce that all other social groups 'form only one reactionary mass' relative to the working class: 'Has one proclaimed to the artisan, small manufacturers, etc., and peasants during the last elections: Relative to us, you, together with the bourgeoisie and feudal lords, form one reactionary mass?' The *Communist Manifesto* had stated: 'the proletariat alone is a really revolutionary class': 'The other classes decay and finally disappear in the face of modern industry.' They may, in their decline be conservative, even reactionary, in their political disposition. Nevertheless, the lower middle class, the small manufacturer, the shopkeeper, the artisan and the peasant were all in various stages of assimilation into the working class and thus potential collaborators (2002: 231). Far from denouncing these different groups as 'one reactionary mass', the *Communist Manifesto* had argued for a broad democratic alliance of the proletariat with other social strata whose economic position was being undermined by industrialization and competition.

One group among these declining social classes was a particular problem for the Left: the peasants. Notoriously, the *Communist Manifesto* had spoken of how urban growth under capitalism had 'rescued a considerable part of the population from the idiocy of rural life'. In the *Eighteenth Brumaire* Marx had compared the French peasantry to a sack of potatoes:

> Each individual peasant family is almost self-sufficient; it directly produces the greater of its own consumption and therefore obtains its means of life more through exchange with nature than through intercourse with society. The smallholding, the peasant, and the family; next door, another smallholding, another peasant and another family. A bunch of these makes up a village, and a bunch of villages makes up a department. Thus the great mass of the French nation is formed by the simple addition of isomorphous magnitudes, much as potatoes in a sack form a sack of potatoes. (1973b: 239)

Volume three of *Capital* was even more scathing in its indictment of the economic inefficiencies and social backwardness of peasant agriculture. It created, Marx said, 'a class of barbarians standing half outside society, combining all the crudity of primitive social forms with all the torments and misery of civilized countries . . .' (1981: 949). Nevertheless, experience of the failed revolutions of 1848 and Louis Napoleon's subsequent coup in France had ensured that Marx was sensitive to the political question of the peasantry. The *Eighteenth Brumaire* had made some careful distinctions between a reactionary, backward-looking peasantry and those 'rebellious peasants' who looked forward to something different. It also provided a sympathetic account of the experience of French peasants under successive regimes which had exploited and oppressed them (1973b: 240–3). In his 1874 notes on Bakunin's *State and Anarchy*, Marx had noted that everywhere in Europe the peasants remained politically significant. The left faced a simple choice:

> either [the peasant] hinders each workers' revolution, makes a wreck of it, as he has formerly done in France, or the proletariat . . . must as government take measures through which the peasant finds his condition immediately improved, so as to win him for the revolution . . . (1974: 334)

Any government of the working class had to ease 'the transition from private ownership of land to collective ownership', securing the peasant's support for the latter 'of his own accord, from economic reasons'. For Marx, the Social Democrats in Germany were doomed to failure unless they took active measures to win the support of the peasants. By the mid-1870s, as we will see, his studies of Russia were leading Marx to revise his assessment of peasant society.

Second, the Gotha Programme also failed to live up to the *Communist Manifesto* on the issue of internationalism. According to the draft programme: 'The working class strives for its emancipation first of all within the framework of the present-day national states, conscious that the necessary result of its efforts, which are common to the workers of all civilized countries, will be the international brotherhood of peoples.' Of course, literally speaking, the nation-state is the immediate arena within which any working class has to act. But, Marx comments, the nation-state is not an autonomous space. Germany, for instance, is interconnected with other capitalist economies and states. The working class must always fight on this wider international terrain too. From their earliest political activities Marx and Engels had been committed to internationalism. Engels, in an article of 1845, 'The Festival of Nations in London', had stressed that 'the proletarians in all countries have one and the same interest, one and the same enemy' (MECW6: 6). The *Communist Manifesto* insisted that the working man has no country and that Communists must always 'bring to the front the common interests of the entire proletariat, independently of all nationality'. 'Workers of the World Unite!' was one of its most famous slogans. In his Inaugural address to the IWMA in 1864, Marx had stressed the political importance of international co-operation: 'Past experience has shown how disregard of that bond of brotherhood which ought to exist between the workmen of different countries, and incite them to stand firmly by each other in all their struggles for emancipation, will be chastised by the common discomfiture of their incoherent efforts' (1974: 81). One of many things about the Paris Commune which impressed Marx was its anti-patriotic spirit in demolishing 'that colossal symbol of martial glory, the Vendome column' (1974: 217).

The case of Ireland was, for Marx, an especially potent instance of the political damage that resulted from the failure to maintain working-class solidarity across national borders. Driven out of Ireland by desperate poverty, especially after the devastating effects of the potato famine in the 1840s, migrant Irish labour flooded into the cities of England and Scotland, increasing the size of the reserve army of labour and dragging down wages. Marx comments, 'in all the major industrial centres of England there is a profound antagonism between the Irish and the English proletarians'. Anti-Irish sentiment was also, he argued, 'artificially kept alive and intensified by the press, the pulpit, the comic papers, in short by all the means at the disposal of the ruling classes (1974: 169). Irish terrorism only intensified this antagonism. For instance, in December 1867 a group of Fenians attempted to liberate some of their leaders from prison in Clerkenwell, London. They made a mess of the whole operation killing several local people, seriously injuring hundreds more and providing a propaganda gift to the British press for a campaign of anti-Irish hysteria. Marx bitterly complained to Engels:

> This latest Fenian exploit in Clerkenwell is a great folly. The London masses, who have shown much sympathy for Ireland, will be enraged by it and driven into the arms of the government party. One cannot expect the London proletarians to let themselves be blown up for the benefit of Fenian emissaries. Secret, melodramatic conspiracies of this kind are, in general, more or less doomed to failure. (MECW42: 501)

Here, for Marx, was a particularly stark instance of the harmful effects of national hostilities and of undemocratic terrorist cliques. The British labour movement must be brought to support Irish independence: 'it is an essential precondition for the emancipation of the English working class to transform the present enforced union . . . into a free and equal confederation, if possible, and into a total separation, if necessary'. This was crucial to the political success of any British revolution (1974: 117–18). National and ethnic tensions divided the working class in many parts of Europe. The IWMA had worked hard in the late 1860s to mitigate such divisions – by, for instance, mobilizing strike support across national borders and by dissuading workers imported to break strikes in England from doing so (1974: 395–6). It also, at Marx's instigation, organized demonstrations of mostly English workers in support of Irish independence. But in the Gotha Programme there was no proper discussion of the international role of the working class and the appropriate strategies to build up effective cross-border co-operation. Instead, there were merely a few pious gestures about 'the international brotherhood of peoples'.

A third issue that concerned Marx was the question of how socialists understood the state. In the Gotha Programme the state was represented as 'an independent entity possessed of its own intellectual, ethical, and libertarian bases', not as an expression of dominant social relations of production (1974: 354). The draft programme had stated: 'The German workers' party, in order to pave the way for the solution of the social question, demands the creation of producers' co-operatives with state aid.' Marx retorts: 'The existing class struggle is discarded in favour of the hack phrase of a newspaper scribbler – "the social question"'. Instead of being the result of a revolutionary process of political and social transformation, the new socialist order 'arises' – Marx places the verb without an active subject in inverted commas – from the financial generosity of the existing state. Marx drily comments: 'The notion that state loans can be used for the construction of a new society as easily as they can for the construction of a new railway is worthy of Lassalle's imagination.' Instead of a revolutionary dictatorship of the proletariat, implementing a series of radical economic and social measures, there is a request for hand-outs from the state and a list of political demands which, Marx says, 'contain nothing beyond the old democratic litany familiar to all: universal suffrage, direct legislation, popular rights, a people's militia, etc.' Keeping 'within the bounds of what is allowed by the police', Marx says, 'the whole programme is thoroughly infested with the Lassallean sect's servile belief in the state' (1974: 353, 355).

Fourth and finally, at first sight of less political relevance, there were critical remarks on several misunderstandings of the labour theory of value. Already in the *German Ideology* those socialists who placed distribution and consumption at the top of the political agenda were sharply criticized. For Marx, production was the essential starting point for any adequate understanding of society: 'if you proceed from production, you necessarily concern yourself with the real conditions of production and with the productive activity of men' (MECW5: 518). Adam Smith and, especially, Ricardo had done this and thus developed real insights into the nature of capitalism. Subsequently most economic writers, including many socialists, had diverted their attention to consumption, distribution, exchange – in other words, to the sphere of circulation, that 'very Eden of the innate rights of man', forgetting about what Marx termed 'the hidden haunts of production, on whose threshold we are faced with the inscription: No admittance except on business'. By ignoring this sphere of work and 'the real relations of production' and focusing instead on the unjust *consequences* of capitalism, socialism becomes largely a matter of how wealth is distributed. The SPD's programme called for 'a fair distribution of the proceeds of labour'. But what, Marx asks, are 'the proceeds of labour' and what is a 'fair distribution?' According to the Gotha Programme, labour is the sole source of wealth. Nature, Marx insisted, is just as important. And its demand that workers should receive the full fruits of their labour is shown to be as rhetorical a gesture as its invocation of 'the international brotherhood of peoples'.

For Marx these misleading claims had significant political ramifications. First, by ignoring the sphere of production the SPD programme did nothing about the brutal exploitation of working men and women in conditions which made human life a living hell and often brought with it chronic illness and premature death. This, as we have seen, was a political issue of overwhelming significance for Marx. Following on from this, the Gotha Programme contained little in the way of serious thinking about the policy issues facing an incoming socialist government. Its aspirations to establish 'a fair distribution of the proceeds of labour' remained no more than an ideal. Thinking seriously about the post-revolutionary distribution of the total product of labour, Marx points to certain necessary deductions: '*First*, cover for replacement of the means of production used up. *Second*, additional portion for expansion of production. *Third*, reserve or insurance funds to provide against accidents, dislocations caused by natural calamities, etc.' Then, further deductions are required. There are the necessary costs of administration. Then there is 'that which is intended for the common satisfaction of needs, such as schools, health services, etc.' And, as Marx goes on to observe, 'this part grows considerably in comparison with present-day society, and it grows in proportion as the new society develops.' Further, there is provision for 'those unable to work, etc., in short, for what is included under so-called official poor relief today.' So the whole notion of the 'fair' distribution to labour of what labour has produced makes no sense and shows a remarkable superficiality in thinking about the economics of socialism – or, for that matter, about the economics of capitalism.

Marx's critical commentary on the Gotha Programme was an uncompromising reassertion both of the revolutionary principles which he and Engels had committed themselves to in the 1840s and of the arguments of *Capital* about the political centrality of the sphere of production.[3] Their relations with the SPD remained strained. In a letter to Engels in October 1877 Marx grumbled about the type of new members who were entering the party: 'a whole gang of half-mature students and super-wise Doctors of Philosophy who want to give socialism a "superior, idealistic" orientation' (1975b: 290). A revolutionary movement or party should consist mainly of workers, as Marx and Engels insisted in their Circular Letter of 1879 attacking the 'three Zurichers'. These three SPD officials had called for the party to abandon talk of revolution and the working class and to become a party of 'independent representatives of science and all men imbued with true love of humanity'. Marx and Engels angrily responded that for nearly forty years they had stressed their commitment to the working class as the agent of 'the modern social revolution':

> When the International was formed, we expressly formulated the battle-cry: the emancipation of the working classes must be conquered by the working classes themselves. We cannot therefore cooperate with people who openly state that the workers are too uneducated to emancipate themselves and must be freed from above by philanthropic big bourgeois and petty bourgeois. (1974: 375)

If a situation like the Berlin revolution of March 1848 should ever occur, where then will these Social Democrats now stand? Presumably they would follow 'the path of legality' and end up clearing away the barricades and marching with the Prussian army 'against the one-sided, coarse, uneducated masses'?[4]

PARLIAMENTARY POLITICS AND REVOLUTION

What then was the later Marx's understanding of the appropriate political strategy for the building of a post-capitalist society? Despite his doubts about the direction the SPD seemed to be heading in, Marx did see a legitimate role for political action within the limits of parliamentary systems. Electoral campaigns and parliamentary debates provided platforms for communicating with the mass of the people, forcing other parties to defend in public their views and actions against socialist criticisms. Whatever its ultimate limitations, participation in parliamentary politics was educative for the working class, which must utilize every political form available to develop its own organizational capacities. More than this, universal suffrage could open the way to long-term social transformation. In 1852 Marx was suggesting that in Britain a peaceful and parliamentary transition to socialism was feasible. Here the proletariat made up the vast majority of the population and 'in a long, though underground civil war, it has gained a clear consciousness of its position as a class'. The six points of its programme, 'the Charter', added up to Universal Suffrage, and this would bring the working class to political power:

> The carrying of Universal Suffrage in England would, therefore, be a far more socialistic measure than anything which has been honored with that name on the Continent. Its inevitable result, here, is *the political supremacy of the working class.* (MECW11: 333)

Marx continued to acknowledge the democratic potential of the bourgeois state, however limited. In speeches to IWMA, he spoke of the importance of electing socialist representatives to parliament where, as in the case of Bebel and Liebknecht in Germany, 'the whole world listens to them'. And he challenged the political indifferentism of one wing of the socialist movement. This was fatal for organized labour which must, he said, seize political power in order 'to construct the new organization of labour' and 'overthrow the old politics which bolster up the old institutions'. However, the strategies to accomplish this are not everywhere the same and he stressed the specificity of political conditions in different parts of Europe. In some countries a peaceful transition via parliamentary elections was possible, at least in principle. In others, however, there was no electoral system and no parliamentary government:

> We know that heed must be paid to the institutions, customs, and traditions of the various countries, and we do not deny that there are countries, such as America, England, and if I was familiar with its institutions, I might include Holland, where the workers may attain their goal by peaceful means. This being the case,

> we must recognize that in most continental countries the lever of the revolution will have to be force; a resort to force will be necessary one day appeal in order to set up the rule of labour. (1974: 324)

According to Engels in his 1886 preface to the first English translation of *Capital*, many years of historical study led Marx to the conclusion that England was the only country, at least in Europe, where 'the inevitable social revolution might be effected entirely by peaceful and legal means.' But Engels added: 'He certainly never forgot to add that he hardly expected the English ruling classes to submit, without a "pro-slavery rebellion," to this peaceful and legal revolution' (1976: 113).

This is a key point. Throughout their long political careers, Marx and Engels were each clear-eyed enough to realize that a peaceful transition to Communism was unlikely. In his 'Principles of Communism' of 1847, Engels had asked the question: Will the peaceful abolition of private property be possible? He replied: 'It would be desirable if this could happen, and the communists would certainly be the last to oppose it.' But he went on to express his scepticism that such a peaceful transition would be possible because of the violence of the defenders of the status quo. Communists, Engels said, saw how any kind of working-class political activity was 'violently suppressed' in many parts of Europe so that 'the opponents of communism have been working toward a revolution with all their strength.' Communists are opposed in principle to insurrectionary adventures, but if the proletariat is finally driven to revolution, then 'we communists will defend the interests of the proletarians with deeds as we now defend them with words' (MECW6: 349–51). This remained Marx's own position on the character of the post-revolution state. Parliamentary representation of labour was always vulnerable to armed intervention by the established order. 'We know you are the armed power which is directed against the proletarians', he warned the governments of Europe; 'we will move against you in peaceful ways where it is possible, and with arms if it should become necessary' (MECW22: 616–17).

Class struggle was not just a matter of popular resistance 'from below'. The history of capitalism outlined in the pages of *Capital* was one in which 'conquest, enslavement, robbery, murder, briefly force, play the great part'. Wealth and a landless labour-force were produced in seventeenth- and eighteenth-century England through the institutions of the state and a good deal of 'brute force'. Property owners used 'the power of the state, the concentrated and organized force of society, to hasten, as in a hothouse, the process of transformation of the feudal mode of production into the capitalist mode, and to shorten the transition' (1976: 915–16). It was, in other words, a kind of dictatorship of the bourgeoisie which created capitalism out of feudalism. And it is the state which continues to sustain the existing mode of production. The *Communist Manifesto* had spoken of 'the more or less veiled civil war, raging within existing society'. And in *Capital* the long struggle for legal restrictions on working hours is described by Marx as 'a civil war of half a century' and 'a protracted civil war, more or less dissembled, between the capitalist class and the working-class.' Ultimately the state was an organization of force for the protection of the interests of the possessing classes. As soon as these interests were significantly threatened, the bourgeoisie would break its own laws and existing constitutional forms. If political reform became social transformation, the reign of legality and democracy would soon end. A violent confrontation between the workers and the ruling powers would soon follow; in short, a revolution – and/or a counter-revolution.

A final point about Marx's conception of revolution. The process of revolution was itself a vital experience in the political education of the working class. Marx and Engels had made this point in the *German Ideology*. Communism, they said, was something that emerged out of real processes. Among those real processes was the alteration of the consciousness of large numbers of people through their experience of revolution: 'this revolution is necessary, therefore, not only because the ruling class cannot be overthrown in any other way, but also because the class overthrowing it can only in a revolution succeed in ridding itself of all the muck of ages and become fitted to found society anew' (MECW5: 88). In other words, through the very process of engaging in revolutionary transformation the working class will itself be transformed. Precisely the same argument was used in the Third Address on the Paris Commune in May, 1871. The working class, Marx said, had no ready-made utopias to impose on society:

> They know that in order to work out their own emancipation, and along with it that higher form to which present society is

irresistibly tending by its own economical agencies, they will have to pass through long struggles, through a series of historic processes, transforming circumstances and men. (MECW23: 336)

TRANSITIONS

Ultimately revolutionary transformation was never simply a product of political will. Larger structural forces generated the crises out of which new political forms would have to be created. Marx was already arguing this in the 1840s. The French Revolution provided no shortage of example of the limitations of the political will he had argued in an important article of 1844: 'The more one-sided – *i.e.*, the more perfect – political understanding is, the more completely it puts its faith in the *omnipotence* of the will, the blinder it is towards the *natural* and spiritual *limitations* of the will, the more incapable it becomes of discovering the real source of the evils of society' (MECW3: 189–206). Thirty years later he is arguing pretty much the same case. The year before his *Critique of the Gotha Programme*, Marx engaged in a critical study of a new book by the great Russian anarchist Bakunin, *Statehood and Anarchy*. Bakunin, he charges, understands only the political language of revolution and 'understands absolutely nothing about social revolution':

> Its economic conditions do not exist for him. As all hitherto existing economic forms, developed or undeveloped, involve the enslavement of the worker (whether in the form of wage-labourer, peasant, etc.), he believes that a *radical revolution* is possible in all such forms alike . . . The *will*, and not the economic conditions, is the foundation of his social revolution. (1974: 334–5)

For Marx, revolutionary politics had always to respond to real economic and social conditions, in a specific place and at a specific time.

A post-capitalist society was not feasible until capitalism had developed to its limits, unleashing the forces of production which created the preconditions for new social relations of production and thus of new forms of distribution of wealth, new kinds of social values and new political forms. Through primitive accumulation capital had created a landless workforce dependent on wage-labour, that is, the working class. Capital's 'historic destiny', Marx said in *Grundrisse*, was only fulfilled when several further conditions had been achieved. The first was the development of needs above and beyond 'mere subsistence, mere use value'. Second, was the creation, through the severe discipline of capital over several generations, of a new kind of labour force. Marx calls them 'a new species'. The third requirement was the development of the productive powers of labour to the point where society requires less and less human labour and more and more work is done by machinery. Capital, in other words, plays a decisive role in creating the conditions for its own supersession. 'This is why', Marx emphasizes, '*capital is productive; i.e., an essential relation for the development of the social productive forces*' (1973c: 324–5).

Through the process of producing new commodities, production also reproduces itself. It produces and reproduces not just commodities and profit, and not just more means of production, but also the core social structure of capitalism itself. In Marx's words: 'it also produces and reproduces the capitalist relation; on the one hand the capitalist, on the other the wage labourer' (1976: 724). However, reproduction is never quite a perfect cycle of repetition, otherwise there would be no change and no history. The productive forces in their deepening conflict with the relations of production themselves do some of the essential work of transition to a post-capitalist society. Socialist forms of production emerge out of the interstices of capitalism. For instance, in the third volume of *Capital* Marx points out that, despite its competitiveness and individualism, capital has developed the 'social powers of production' through co-operation and the division of labour, even if at this stage the capitalist minority pocket all of its fruits. These latter are, he says, the 'trustees of bourgeois society' and he goes on to discuss joint-stock companies. These large enterprises, in which the former capitalist owner has become a manager, represent 'the abolition of capital as private property within the framework of capitalist production itself'. They are, in other words, steps towards the socialization of bourgeois property. This is, Marx goes on:

> a necessary point of transition towards the transformation of capital back into the property of producers, though no longer as the private property of individual producers, but rather as their property as associated producers, as directly social property. (1981: 568)

Another emergent form of socialized production was the working-class co-operative of various kinds, which Marx says, 'represent within the old form the first sprouts of the new'. Always sceptical about utopian projects for overcoming capitalism, Marx notes how these co-operatives 'naturally reproduce in all cases, in their present organisation, all the defects of the existing system'. Nevertheless they too are important transitional forms of economic organization. Joint-stock companies and worker co-operatives are two forms of transition from the capitalist mode of production to what he terms 'the associated one' (1981: 571–2).

Is a gradual and peaceful transition to socialism feasible on the basis of economic and social development? The first volume of *Capital* closes on a surprisingly positive note, suggesting that the transition from capitalism to communism will be more rapid and considerably less painful than the transition from feudalism to capitalism:

> The transformation of scattered private property resting on the personal labour of the individuals themselves into capitalist private property is naturally an incomparably more protracted, violent, and difficult process than the transformation of capitalist private property, which in fact rests on the carrying on of production by society, into social property. In the former case, it was a matter of the expropriation of the mass of the people by a few usurpers; but in this case, we have the expropriation of a few usurpers by the mass of the people. (1976: 929–30)

However, the main thrust of Marx's argument, in *Grundrisse* and in *Capital*, is less optimistic and points precisely towards 'a protracted, violent, and difficult process'. Increasing incompatibility between the drive to develop the forces of production and the existing social relations of production, generates a series of crises and short term resolutions.

In chapter 32 of *Capital* there is a powerful and widely quoted narrative of how this process of internal self-destruction will (or might) work itself out. On the one hand there is the growth of a whole array of productive forces, pushing beyond private capitalism – 'the growth of the co-operative form of the labour process, the conscious technical application of science, the planned exploitation of the soil, the transformation of the means of labour into forms in which they can only be used in common', and so on. There is also the growth of the world-market and the international character of the capitalist regime. At the same time there is increasing centralization of capital into fewer hands and the generation of overwhelming anti-capitalist forces:

> Along with the constant decrease in the number of capitalist magnates, who usurp and monopolize all advantages of this process of transformation, the mass of misery, oppression, slavery, degradation and exploitation grows; but with this there also grows the revolt of the working-class, a class constantly increasing in numbers, and trained, united, organized by the very mechanism of the capitalist process of production. The monopoly of capital becomes a fetter upon the mode of production, which has flourished alongside and under it. The centralization of the means of production and socialization of labour reach a point at which they become incompatible with their capitalist integument. This integument is burst asunder. The knell of capitalist private property sounds. The expropriators are expropriated. (1976: 929)

This passage raises several important issues. The so-called 'immiseration thesis', the comment that 'the mass of misery, oppression, slavery, degradation and exploitation grows', will be picked up and discussed further in the next chapter. Here I want to explore further the nature of the structural crisis which destabilizes the capitalist mode of production? Though 'a lack of effective demand or effective consumption' (1978: 486), is one dimension of the endemic crisis, Marx rejects explanations which depend upon some kind of 'underconsumptionist' thesis – that economic crises are caused by a lack of purchasing power of the working class. The *Grundrisse* had already pointed to the tendency of the rate of profit to decline as the crucial mechanism of capitalist instability. Surplus value depends on the ratio of surplus, or unpaid, labour to paid, or necessary labour. But as the forces of production develop, via mechanization for instance, the role played by workers decreases. So the rate of profit decreases. For Marx this is 'the most important law of modern political economy' (1973c: 748). This is pursued further in three chapters in the third volume of *Capital* which investigate what he called 'the law of the tendency of the rate of profit to fall'. This is a long and complex discussion but the upshot is – that as fixed capital increases relative to the amount of living labour employed, so necessarily the rate of profit will tend to fall, though there are countervailing tendencies at work. In other words, there is a falling ratio of surplus value to capital. This in turn, Marx says, 'promotes overproduction, speculation and crises, and leads to the existence of excess capital alongside excess population' (1981: 350). Such crises are endemic to capitalism. However, as Marx notes later, they create the conditions for their own, temporary, resolution. Falls in wages and prices, bitter competition, the destruction of some sectors of capital in various industries, leads to the introduction of greater efficiency via the introduction of machinery. After a period of depression and stagnation a new phase of expansion begins: 'And so we go round the whole circle once again' (1981: 364).

But the cycle was not destined to go round and round for ever. The tendency of the rate of profit to fall had been a matter of concern to Ricardo and of horror among contemporary political economists. It was an evident barrier to the further development of the productive forces and Marx triumphantly comments:

> [T]his characteristic barrier in fact testifies to the restrictiveness and the solely historical and transitory character of the capitalist mode of production; it bears witness that this is not an absolute mode of production for the production of wealth but actually comes into conflict at a certain stage with the latter's further development. (1981: 350)

These cyclical crises are part of the roller-coaster pattern of development of industrial capitalism. But at the core of the process is this irremovable barrier of the problem of profit. The resolution of each crisis is temporary and merely postpones the day of reckoning. As Marx had put it succinctly in *Grundrisse*, 'these regularly recurring catastrophes lead to their repetition on a higher scale, and finally to its violent overthrow' (1973c: 750).

Returning to the passage in which Marx anticipates the sound of 'the knell of capitalist private property', it is worth noting the inclusion, alongside structural crisis, of political *action*. Revolution is represented in structural terms – as an incompatibility between the increasingly collectivist character of the forces of production and the private capitalist character of the relations of production. But in response to deepening social polarization and economic crisis, a political subject – the working class – actively revolts against its material impoverishment and its inhuman treatment. This is the language of radical politics – 'revolt' against 'slavery' and 'oppression', though also including the distinctively socialist term 'exploitation'. Note that this class has been 'trained, united, organized' by the process of capitalist production itself. It is a political subject but one formed within the economic sphere of production and itself an effect of the structural crisis.

EVOLUTION AND PROGRESS

Is it the case that capitalism must fulfil its 'historic destiny' before any kind of transformation can be brought about through political action? Must all societies endure the successive brutalities of slavery, serfdom, primitive accumulation and industrialization? In 1861 Marx was reading Appian's *Civil Wars of Rome* (in the original Greek). 'Spartacus emerges as the most capital fellow in the whole history of antiquity', he told Engels. 'A great general (no Garibaldi he), of noble character, a *real representative* of the proletariat of ancient times' (MECW41: 264). For Marx, Spartacus was a heroic figure in his resistance to the brutalities of slavery in the Roman world. At the same time, however, he argued that slavery was a major step forward in the development of the forces and relations of production in the ancient world. The labour of hundreds of thousands of slaves provided the material foundations of the cultural and intellectual achievements of Greece and Rome. Engels put the issues succinctly in *Anti-Duhring* in 1877 – and there is no reason to think that Marx would have dissented from this judgement. It is very easy to denounce slavery, Engels says. This does no more than state the obvious – that the institutions of the ancient world, including slavery, are no longer appropriate to modern conditions of life.[5] High moral indignation does nothing to explain why slavery emerged when and where it did or to enable us to understand its historical significance. If we think about these questions, Engels says, 'we are compelled to say – however contradictory and heretical it may sound – that the introduction of slavery under the conditions prevailing at that time was a great step forward'. He explains:

> It was slavery that first made possible the division of labour between agriculture and industry on a larger scale, and thereby also

> Hellenism, the flowering of the ancient world. Without slavery, no Greek state, no Greek art and science, without slavery, no Roman Empire. But without the basis laid by Hellenism and the Roman Empire, also no modern Europe. We should never forget that our whole economic, political and intellectual development presupposes a state of things in which slavery was as necessary as it was universally recognised. In this sense we are entitled to say: Without the slavery of antiquity no modern socialism. (MECW25: 168–9)

On the one hand slavery is an appalling and degrading institution and those who bitterly opposed it, like Spartacus, are to be celebrated. On the other hand, as a form of organizing labour it was an important and valuable step forward on the long road to the ultimate liberation of humanity from scarcity.

If we turn back to Marx's account of 'Primitive Accumulation' in *Capital*, we find a similarly bifurcated response to historical change and to 'progress'. On the one hand his writing is suffused with indignation. The very title of one of the key chapters is unambiguous: 'Bloody Legislation Against the Expropriated, from the End of the 15th Century. Forcing Down of Wages by Acts of Parliament'. Peasants and yeomen farmers were thrown off the land by the legal chicanery of enclosures or via the more brutal 'clearances' in Scotland and Ireland. As dispossessed free labourers they were treated by the law as voluntary criminals. 'The fathers of the present working-class were chastised for their enforced transformation into vagabonds and paupers', Marx comments and details the brutal disciplining of this 'free' proletariat under successive English monarchs. In 1530, during the time of Henry VIII, for instance, those who refused to work were whipped on the first offence, mutilated on the second, and executed on the third as enemies of the state. Similar legislation against vagrants, beggars and vagabonds was enacted throughout the next two centuries. 'Thus were the agricultural folk first forcibly expropriated from the soil, driven from their homes, turned into vagabonds, and then whipped, branded and tortured by grotesquely terroristic laws into accepting the discipline necessary for the system of wage-labour' (1976: 899).

This long and brutal process was, Marx says, essential to lay down the foundation of modern capitalism and thus of a Communist future. Only free labour created the opportunity for the massive expansion of productive capacity visible in the huge wealth of mid-Victorian Britain. *The Communist Manifesto* voiced this in dramatic form:

> The bourgeoisie, during its rule of scarce one hundred years, has created more massive and more colossal productive forces than have all preceding generations together. Subjection of Nature's forces to man, machinery, application of chemistry to industry and agriculture, steam-navigation, railways, electric telegraphs, clearing of whole continents for cultivation, canalisation of rivers, whole populations conjured out of the ground – what earlier century had even a presentiment that such productive forces slumbered in the lap of social labour? (2002: 224–5)

Doesn't Marx both have has his cake and eat it here? In the detailed histories of the present which occupy several chapters of the first volume of *Capital* – 'primitive accumulation' and 'industrial revolution' – Marx denounces the bourgeoisie as the agent of historical changes which brutalized generations of working people. At the same time, he represents these changes as progressive, creating the essential foundations for a better future.

This, for Marx, is the tragedy of history: 'the development of the richness of human nature' requires 'the development of human productive forces' though this often involves the wholesale destruction of traditions, ancient ways of life, civilizations. It also involves the sacrifice of real individuals. Marx thus underwrites Ricardo's support for capitalism against his 'sentimental opponents'. Only through the development of the productive forces can 'the development of the richness of human nature as an end in itself' be achieved:

> To oppose the welfare of the individual to this end, as Sismondi does, is to assert that the development of the species must be arrested in order to safeguard the welfare of the individual, so that, for instance, no war may be waged in which at all events some individuals perish . . . Apart from the barrenness of such edifying reflections, they reveal a failure to understand the fact that, although at first the development of the capacities of the human species takes place at the cost of the majority of human individuals and even classes, in the end it breaks through this contradiction and coincides with the development of the individual;

> the higher development of individuality is thus only achieved by a historical process during which individuals are sacrificed . . .[6]

Ricardo's 'ruthlessness' was, according to Marx, 'scientifically honest' and he pursued it with remorseless rigour irrespective of where it led. Marx too is confident that, whatever the short-term costs, the ultimate destination of the painful transformations effected by primitive accumulation and industrialization was a future in which, for the first time in human history, exploitation, oppression, poverty and hunger would no longer exist.

This raises difficult ethical and political questions. Read as a statement about the realities of the historical past, this is a tragic recognition of the painful but inevitable costs of progress – though perhaps troubling in its confidence. What is much more troubling is to read this – especially the final sentence – as a justification of human sacrifice in the present for some promised future. So-called 'socialist primitive accumulation' under Stalin provides one example of how Marx's comments on historical periodization can be read in ways that justify the most pitiless social policies in the name of necessity and progress.

These problems surface in particularly acute and controversial form if we look at two famous, even notorious newspaper articles written by Marx in 1853: 'The British Rule in India' and 'The Future Results of British Rule in India'. The first speaks positively of the opening up of the traditional Indian village to the competitive demands of the world market: 'sickening as it must be to human feeling to witness those myriads of industrious patriarchal and inoffensive social organizations disorganized and dissolved into their units, thrown into a sea of woes, and their individual members losing at the same time their ancient form of civilization and their hereditary means of subsistence'. But, he goes on point out that these village communities were the solid foundation of Oriental Despotism with its caste divisions, its slavery, its religious superstitions and backward-looking traditions. So whatever the intentions of British colonialism, its effects were ultimately progressive:

> England, it is true, in causing a social revolution in Hindustan, was actuated only by the vilest interests, and was stupid in her manner of enforcing them. But that is not the question. The

> question is, can mankind fulfil its destiny without a fundamental revolution in the social state of Asia? If not, whatever may have been the crimes of England, she was the unconscious tool of history in bringing about that revolution. (2007: 218–19)

Marx had no nostalgia for the passing of traditional ways of doing things and was always hostile to backward-looking utopias. Only the revolutionary transformations generated by capitalism created the possibility for a better future.

'Wealth does not appear as the aim of production' in the ancient world, Marx says in *Grundrisse*, looking at attitudes towards property in ancient Rome. Other values, to do with citizenship and status, had a higher priority. On the face of it this seems, Marx says, 'very lofty when contrasted to the modern world, where production appears as the aim of mankind and wealth as the aim of production'. But if 'the childish world of antiquity' was loftier in this respect, it remained locked within its own limits. And Marx goes on to celebrate the potential of increasing production under capitalism with an enthusiasm equal to anything in the *Communist Manifesto*:

> when the limited bourgeois form is stripped away, what is wealth other than the universality of individual needs, capacities, pleasures, productive forces etc., created through universal exchange? The full development of human mastery over the forces of nature, those of so-called nature as well as of humanity's own nature? The absolute working-out of his creative potentialities, with no presupposition other than the previous historic development, which makes this totality of development, i.e. the development of all human powers as such the end in itself, not as measured on a *predetermined yardstick?* (1973c: 488)

Later in the same section of *Grundrisse* Marx talks about how under the medieval guild system artisan work involved a degree of creative and artistic expression (1973c: 497). But he does not permit himself any nostalgia about the lost world of medieval craftsmen – in the way that his contemporary John Ruskin in works like *The Stones of Venice* did. As we have seen already in Chapter 3, in his account of industrialization in *Capital* Marx documents the deskilling of labour, the relentless destruction of craft skills, the brutalized working conditions and declining real incomes of workers. At the same time he represents industrialization as, in the long term, a positive force.

However the potential of capitalist production is assessed, and later Marxists have been less sanguine than Marx and sometimes as pessimistic as Ruskin, the question remains: must the path opened up by industrial capitalism in Britain be necessarily followed by other societies? In the preface to the first edition of volume one of *Capital,* complacent German readers were warned that 'the natural laws of capitalist production' work themselves out 'with iron necessity': 'The country that is more developed industrially only shows, to the less developed, the image of its own future' (1976: 91). In chapter 26 the expropriation of the English peasantry and creation of a landless rural labour-force is represented as a process inevitably repeated in all the countries of Western Europe. But here Marx qualifies his argument: 'The history of this expropriation assumes different aspects in different countries, and runs through its various phases in different orders of succession, and at different historical epochs' (1976: 876). Now the English case is, he says, exceptional though it is also 'the classic form' of the process. It is difficult here to understand precisely what 'classic form' means. Is the English case unique or exemplary? How significant are the differences in historical sequence from country to country? Are we looking at a single underlying process which simply takes different national forms? Are we looking at one history or several histories? Confusion seems unavoidable for even the attentive reader and, in a letter (unsent) of November 1877, Marx reprimands one of them for extrapolating his account to Russia:

> He insists on transforming my historical sketch of the genesis of capitalism in Western Europe into an historico-philosophic theory of the general path of development prescribed by fate to all nations, whatever the historical circumstances in which they find themselves . . . (1975b: 293)

The account in *Capital* has become merely a 'historical sketch' and 'iron necessity', 'natural' or inevitable laws of development, and all the rest are downplayed. Instead, it is 'historical circumstances' that now play a crucial determining role.

Marx concludes this long and important letter of 1877 with a discussion of another well-known case which could not be fitted into any kind of rigid sequence of historical stages. The dispossession of the free peasants of ancient Rome gave rise not to capitalism but to slavery:

> Thus events strikingly analogous but taking place in different historical surroundings led to totally different results. By studying each of these forms of evolution separately and then comparing them one can easily find the clue to this phenomenon, but one will never arrive there by using as one's master key a general historico-philosophical theory, the supreme virtue of which consists in being supra-historical. (1975b: 294)

This is just one of a number of instances in which the austere logic of the 1859 'Preface' and some of Marx's other formulations about historical necessity are questioned and qualified when Marx changes focus, engages with problems of historical specificity and examines particular processes of change.

LATE MARX AND RUSSIA

In recent years new readings of 'late Marx', especially his preoccupation with the recent history of Russia, have taken these questions further. Was Marx in the 1870s beginning to rethink some of his own core theses about historical stages and political transitions?

The *Communist Manifesto* had had little to say about Russia, perceived by radicals as the headquarters of European reaction in the first half of the nineteenth century. Their internationalism was severely tested by a degree of Slavophobia, especially after the reactionary role of the peasantry in the revolutions of 1848 across Eastern Europe.[7] Under pressure of the immediate political situation, Marx and Engels abandoned their own theoretical method – rigorous economic and social analysis of political movements. Unable to understand why the peasantry moved towards various forms of nationalism and conservatism, Marx and Engels fell back on the Hegelian device of writing off the 'Slavs' as 'non-historic peoples'. After 1848 Marx continued to identify Russia in particular as a backward semi-feudal social and political order which must go through much the same historical experiences as had the more advanced capitalist states of Western Europe. When Alexander II supported plans for the emancipation of the serfs in 1859, Marx immediately saw parallels to the crisis of the *ancien régime* in France in the previous century. As in France in 1789, so in Russia in 1859, the whole regime was beginning to fall apart as new forces of production began to transform the social and political relations of production. A Russian Jacobin regime was at hand:

> the nobility are sure to resist; the Emperor, tossed about between state necessity and expediency, between fear of the nobles and fear of the enraged peasants, is sure to vacillate; and the serfs, with expectations worked up to the highest pitch, and with the idea that the Czar is for them, but held down. by the nobles, are surer than ever to rise. And if they do, the Russian 1793 will be at hand; the reign of terror of these half-Asiatic serfs will be something unequaled in history; but it will be the second turning point in Russian history, and finally place real and general civilization in the place of that sham and show introduced by Peter the Great. (MECW16: 147)

During the 1860s and 70s the political significance of Russia for the rest of Europe continued to draw the attention of Marx and Engels. They continued to see contemporary Russia in terms of *ancien-régime* France, predicting a revolution of a similar kind. In a letter of April 1879 to Nikolai Danielson, translator of *Capital* into Russian, Marx was still arguing this. Russia's rocky state finances and increasing bankruptcy, he said, 'reminds you rather of the time of Louis XIV and Louis XV, where the financial, commercial, industrial superstructure, or rather the facades of the social edifices, looked (although they had a much more solid foundation than in Russia) like a satyre upon the stagnant state of the bulk of production (the agricultural one) and the famine of the producers' (1975b: 299–300).

However, during the 1870s Marx was also rethinking his assumptions about the necessity either of a bourgeois revolution or of the transformation of peasant Russia, via primitive accumulation, into a fully fledged capitalist society. He learned Russian, studied all kinds of official sources and began to ponder the feasibility of a direct transition from the traditional Russian village community to socialism. In 1877 he responded to some Russian criticisms of his work with a forthright rejection of the arguments of Russian liberals that the communal property of the peasants must be destroyed and the development of capitalism accelerated. 'I have arrived at this result', he stated: 'if Russia continues along the path it has followed since 1861, it will miss the finest chance that history has ever offered a nation, only to undergo all the fatal vicissitudes of the capitalist system' (1975: 292). And to another Russian correspondent Marx wrote in 1881 explaining why Russia could avoid the European experience of the expropriation of the peasantry and the creation of a propertyless working class:

> Because in Russia, thanks to a unique combination of circumstances, the rural commune, still established on a nationwide scale, may gradually detach itself from its primitive features and develop directly as an element of collective production on a nationwide scale. It is precisely thanks to its contemporaneity with capitalist production that it may appropriate the latter's *positive acquisitions* without experiencing all its frightful misfortunes. (MECW24: 346)

The common ownership of land allows the Russian village community to transform individualist farming into co-operative farming while taking advantage of the new possibilities of large-scale mechanical cultivation. As Marx says: 'it can turn over a new leaf without beginning by committing suicide'. However, if this was true in principle, in practice the picture was not so encouraging. Powerful forces were at work undermining the traditional peasant commune:

> [T]oday the very existence of the Russian commune has been jeopardised by a conspiracy of powerful interests; crushed by the direct extortions of the State, fraudulently exploited by the 'capitalist' intruders, merchants, etc., and the land 'owners', it is undermined, into the bargain, by the village usurers, by conflicts of interests provoked in its very heart by the situation prepared for it. (MECW24: 349)

Only one thing could save the Russian commune – a revolution: 'If revolution comes at the opportune moment, if it concentrates all its forces so as to allow the rural commune full scope, the latter will soon develop as an element of regeneration in Russian society and an element of superiority over the countries enslaved by the capitalist system' (MECW24: 349). Note that Marx suggests here that the rural commune could provide a post-revolutionary agent of change superior to anything in the capitalist West. However, at the same time, this was feasible only because of technologies imported from the capitalist West.

In their preface to a new Russian edition of the *Communist Manifesto*, dated January 1882, Marx and Engels returned to the question of whether Russia must follow the same processes of historical development as had happened in Western Europe. Could it avoid the generations of suffering required to pass through the capitalist stage and move directly into socialism? Their reply was cagey: 'If the Russian Revolution becomes the signal for a proletarian revolution in the West, so that both complement each other, the present Russian common ownership of land may serve as the starting point for a communist development' (2002: 196). In other words, the answer was – 'perhaps', if revolution in Russia was reinforced by socialist revolution among the advanced capitalist societies of the West.

Marx's late work on Russia has attracted some attention in recent years. A number of commentators have seen it as a break from, or at least a significant modification of the core positions developed by Marx since the *German Ideology* and especially the stress on capitalism as a progressive force and a necessary stage in providing the foundations of a Communist future. Is there a significant discontinuity between the Marx of *Capital* and this 'later Marx' – less optimistic about the potential for Communism in the years after the defeat of the Paris Commune and the collapse of IWMA, more open to other paths towards a post-capitalist future? Did the 'laws' of historical materialism apply only to countries in Western Europe, similar in their history to England? Could Russia skip the painful experiences of primitive accumulation and industrialization and leap directly into Communism? Marx's Russian studies opened up a debate about alternative paths of development and about the value of pre-capitalist survivals in creating a new kind of society.[8] It was a debate that was particularly important for twentieth-century Marxism in the aftermath first of the Russian revolution, then of the Chinese revolution in 1949 and then of the upsurge of anti-imperialist struggles in various parts of Asia, Africa and Latin America in the 1950s and 60s.

CONCLUSION

In key respects the arguments of these political interventions by Marx in the 1870s point in a number of different directions. Marx did not work out a coherent theory of the transition. Very different, even divergent arguments can be found here – and scattered throughout his writings. Several basic principles do remain constant. First, Marx elaborated analyses of concrete contemporary and historical processes. He did *not* provide a code of revolutionary political practice aimed at establishing an ideal society. Nor did he produce a set of rules for use by parties and elites seeking power. Having said that, in various kinds of writing, often arising out of his own direct experience in the 1860s and 70s, he had important political points to make. Parliamentary political activity was of some value, though he was sceptical that it could lead to a peaceful transition to socialism. A democratically elected government committed to socialist policies would soon discover the limits of parliamentary power. Once real inroads were made on the power and wealth of the minority, organized labour would be confronted by the forces of the established order, including the armed forces, and violence would ensue. Here again Marx is consistent. His attitude towards the state remained unremittingly hostile, from his work in the mid-1840s until his final writings nearly forty years later. It was not this or that aspect of the state which was the problem. Nor did any kind of reform of the state offer a solution. The state itself was the problem. As he had written in his account of the Paris Commune in 1871:

> This was, therefore, a revolution not against this or that, Legitimate, Constitutional, Republican or Imperialist form of state power. It was a revolution against the *state* itself, this supernaturalist abortion of society, a resumption by the people for the people of its own social life. It was not a revolution to transfer it from one fraction of the ruling classes to another, but a revolution to break down this horrid machinery of class domination itself. (1974: 249)

Similarly at the socio-economic level, the development of transitional post-capitalist forces and relations of production pointed forward to a new order. Elements of collective ownership of the means of production and co-operative forms of organization were emerging out of capitalist development. But the potential for peaceful and gradual transition would inevitably be intercepted by deeper and deeper economic crises and, ultimately, catastrophic collapse. The importance of Marx's writings here, as elsewhere, is not in his answers but in the difficult and uncompromising questions he poses.

CHAPTER 7

CONCLUSION: AFTER CAPITALISM

> *Capital, which has such 'good reasons' for denying the sufferings of the legions of workers surrounding it, allows its actual movement to be determined as much and as little by the sight of the coming degradation and final depopulation of the human race, as by the probable fall of the sun into the earth. In every stock-jobbing swindle every one knows that at some time or other the crash must come, but everyone hopes that it may fall on the head of his neighbour, after he himself has caught the shower of gold and placed it in secure hands. Apres moi le deluge! is the watchword of every capitalist and every capitalist nation. Capital therefore takes no account of the health and the length of life of the worker, unless society forces it to do so.*
>
> *(1976: 381)*

One of the conventional criticisms of projects for a radical transformation of society is that they end up as regimes more doctrinaire and authoritarian than those they replaced. It is difficult to forget the concluding lines of George Orwell's *Animal Farm*. The revolution of the animals against the cruelty of men has led to an equally cruel regime of pigs who now associate with men, not with animals: 'The creatures outside looked from pig to man, and from man to pig, and from pig to man again; but already it was impossible to say which was which.' And so an old conservative message is reaffirmed. No matter how attractive radical visions of a new social order, the crooked timbers of humanity are resistant to being straightened. And when the representatives of the new order find their radical vision being resisted by such irrationality, then the new order is imposed with increasing force and rigour. Robespierre and the Jacobin's reign of terror exemplify the authoritarianism at the heart of the Enlightenment; Stalinism represents the authoritarian core of Marxism. This kind of argument goes back at least as far as Edmund Burke's *Reflections on the Revolution in France* – his 1790 polemic against the French Revolution and its English supporters.

But as we have seen, Marx was equally hostile to utopian projects and to doctrinaire political intellectuals. And he was always averse to speculation about what kind of post-capitalist society would emerge out of the profound economic, social and political upheavals which he posited as its essential preconditions. He took evident pleasure from criticisms in a French positivist journal that *Capital* confined itself 'to the critical analysis of the actual facts, instead of writing recipes . . . for the cook-shops of the future' (1976: 99). The conviction that the new order would be shaped precisely by the specific historical conditions of the time and place of the revolution – and by the revolutionary process itself – is present in Marx's writing from first to last. As the sixth of the *Theses on Feuerbach* had stated, there is no inherent human nature, no single 'essence of human': 'the human essence is no abstraction inherent in each single individual. In its reality it is the ensemble of social relations' (1975a: 423). In other words, the essence of man is that there is no essence of man, but instead a set of internalized social relations which are historically variable. What Marx described as the 'working-out of his creative potentialities', can therefore have no presuppositions, apart from specific historical examples. And these display remarkable variation. Thus any detailed elaboration of a future society would necessarily be highly speculative. Marx's later formulations of this principle were more directly political. A post-capitalist future will not be created 'from above', by realizing the ideals and visions of intellectuals and political cliques. It will be built by the working class themselves out of the material, economic and social conditions in which they find themselves. The preface to the 1872 German edition of the *Communist Manifesto* noted the dramatic the transformations of society that had taken place since its first publication and how different the political landscape now was within which new forms of working-class organization had to operate. The general principles laid down 1848 remained sound, but many of the detailed policies and strategies were no longer relevant: 'The practical application of the principles will depend, as the *Manifesto* itself states, everywhere and at all times, on the historical conditions for the time being existing . . .' (2002: 193–4). And therefore, they go on to say, no special stress should be placed on the specific revolutionary measures which they proposed in 1848.

LABOUR

Having said that, it is not difficult to see in broad outline the kind of post-capitalist world which Marx anticipated and supported. It is already suggested very concisely in the *Communist Manifesto.* Initially, a strongly centralized state socialism in which all land and all the main industries were in public control and in which the surplus value generated by labour was recycled for the benefit of all; this would then give way to an increasingly apolitical and stateless social order, characterized by the end of exploitation, of overwork and of poverty.

Marx occasionally allows himself a few utopian projections. Probably the best known is the image in the *German Ideology* of a life beyond the division of labour:

> He is a hunter, a fisherman, a shepherd, or a critical critic, and must remain so if he does not want to lose his means of livelihood; while in communist society, where nobody has one exclusive sphere of activity, but each one can become accomplished in any branch he wishes, society regulates the general production and makes it possible for me to do one thing today and another tomorrow, to hunt in the morning, fish in the afternoon, rear cattle in the evening, criticize after dinner, without ever becoming hunter, fisherman, shepherd, or critic. (MECW5: 46)

The many-sided individual of communist society would be the antithesis of modern man, whose creativity has been distorted by specialization, a consequence of the division of labour. Marx's pastoral vision here is uncharacteristically pre-modern. Hunters, fishermen, shepherds are not exactly at the cutting edge of industrial progress. Can he be a marine engineer in the morning, a computer programmer in the afternoon, a bus driver in the evening and a film director after dinner?

Whatever the answer to that question, the issue of work remains a major contemporary issue, though it also remains a hidden sphere. The situation of the factory worker had been the focus of Marx's attention in substantial sections of *Capital*. Chapter 15, 'Machinery and Large-Scale Industry', at nearly 150 pages long, was the size of a short book. As we saw in Chapter 4, Marx stressed how industrial development not only increased the productivity of labour but also increased its intensity and the negative effects on the body and mind of the labourer. The experience of the factory floor was one of physical pain, damage to the senses and danger:

> Every sense organ is injured by the artificially high temperatures, by the dust-laden atmosphere, by the deafening noise, not to mention the danger to life and limb among machines which are so closely crowded together, a danger which, with the regularity of the seasons, produces its list of those killed and wounded in the industrial battle. (1976: 552)

The factory worker is deprived of what is necessary for life – light and fresh air, protection against the dangerous side-effects of the production process, time for rest and recuperation. For Marx the materialist, the sensuous experience of labour is important, but so too is the intellectual and emotional dimension of work: 'Factory work exhausts the nervous system to the uttermost; at the same time it does away with the many-sided play of the muscles and confiscates every atom of freedom, both in bodily and in intellectual activity' (1976: 548). The new machinery, by destroying the traditional skills of the craftsman, removes the conscious engagement of the worker with what he, or she, is doing. He thus loses his freedom as a human being, becoming a mere appendage of a machine. Even the lightening of the manual element becomes 'an instrument of torture', since it deprives the work of any meaningful content, reducing it to pointless repetition.

The issue of the experience of work, which Marx placed at the centre of the political agenda, is as crucial today. For most people paid work is a major part of their lives – it occupies most of their waking hours for at least five days a week and for most of their adult lives. They/we have to work to generate an income to pay for essential material goods – clothing, food, housing (including heat and light). The alternative is 'unemployment' – a condition which not only drags income down to a bare minimum but subjects individuals to degrading and humiliating conditions to procure that minimum from the state. On the one side, there is too much work – too many hours of the day, leaving too little energy to do much else but get home, cook a meal, and rest. On the other hand, there is too little work, leading to physical, mental and social impoverishment. There are no funds for anything much beyond basics. And a lack of money and of the sociability of the workplace can easily lead to social isolation, loneliness and depression. Overwork or lack of work: are these really the only alternatives? And what kind of work?

What is wealth for any individual, Marx asks, if it isn't in some way 'the working out of his creative potentials' (1973: 488). But under capitalism, as under other modes of production, only a minority are provided with the free time necessary for this creative activity.

> Just as plants live from the earth, and animals live from the plants or plant-eating animals, so does the part of society which possesses free time, disposable time not absorbed in the direct production of subsistence, live from the surplus labour of the workers. Wealth is therefore disposable time. (MECW31: 105–6)

Culture, in its bourgeois form, is purchased at the cost of the workers, Marx says. They are forced to sacrifice everything which characterizes the good life, even life itself, in long hours of painful and mind-numbing wage-labour. 'The working class represents lack of development in order that other classes can represent human development', Marx comments (MECW32: 799). This is the painful irony of capitalist accumulation: it is based on the physical and mental suffering of those who are excluded from many of the creative possibilities opened up by their own labour. Like the oarsmen in Homer's *The Odyssey*, deafened to the songs of the Sirens, they are condemned to row Odysseus's boat relentlessly on.[1]

For Marx work is not necessarily a painful or tedious form of activity. His early writings – especially the *Economic and Philosophical Manuscripts* of 1844 – had emphasized how human beings are by nature active and productive. Animals produce, but only to satisfy their own immediate needs and those of their young. Human beings, however, produce not just to meet their material needs but to fulfil a variety of creative and social needs. 'The practical creation of an objective world, the fashioning of organic nature', is how Marx summarizes the ultimate purpose of human labour. It is the means by which humanity creates and recreates itself as something more than just a needy animal. Is it utopian to suggest that there are non-alienated forms of work which are creative and enjoyable? Surely we can identify such forms of labour all around us? I often bake my own bread. I buy my raw materials and follow different recipes. The bread eventually fills the house with the most wonderful smells. It tastes wonderful too and I delight to share it with family and friends. Their enjoyment of it gives me pleasure. But when I was a student I worked in a large bakery for four long summers: mostly 12-hour night shifts of hard and tedious labour. The bread produced was not mine and its production had neither interest nor pleasure for me. For several years after, my heart sank whenever I encountered the smell of bread baking. Everyone can point to their own experiences of non-alienated labour – creative work that brings pleasure and delight which is both individual and shared. Gardening must be one the most widespread examples today? But of course, the pleasures and the rewards of such forms of labour as working in the garden, or playing the piano, or baking bread or even writing a book about Marx are one thing. Co-ordinating the running of a large power station, laying bricks for a wall on a cold winter morning, driving a double-decker bus through a busy city centre are something else – and unlikely to provide the same kinds of rewards.

Labour is the permanent condition of human existence. In all forms of society and all periods of history, whatever the mode of production, human beings must wrestle with nature to satisfy essential material needs. This is the realm of necessity. Far from civilization reducing these human needs, it expands them and thus the realm of necessity expands. But, at the same time, capital, especially via the development of machines, has now created the necessary conditions for 'the general reduction of the necessary labour of society to a minimum' and thus 'to free everyone's time for their own development'. The exclusion of the working class majority from creative activity is increasingly obsolete. In a post-capitalist society, Marx says, 'disposable time will grow for all'. More than this, capital creates the material preconditions for 'the rich individuality which is as all-sided in its production as in its consumption, and whose labour also therefore appears no longer as labour, but as the full development of activity itself'. In other words, drudgery will be performed by machines and work will become a pleasurable and fulfilling activity (1973: 706, 708).

> Freedom, in this sphere, can consist only in this, that socialized man, the associated producers, govern the human metabolism with nature in a rational way, bringing it under their collective control, instead of being dominated by it as a blind power; accomplishing it with the least expenditure of energy and in conditions most worthy and appropriate for their human nature. (1981: 959)

So Marx is not proposing some kind of socialist work ethic through which drudgery for an employer is merely replaced by drudgery working for the collective good. It is not just capitalist exploitation that makes work alienating, but the reduction of life to painful and pointless activity – irrespective of the size of the wage or who is the employer. The point is to reduce the amount of work through the application of technical knowledge.[2] For Marx, then, the negative aspects of some necessary types of work can be mitigated in a post-capitalist society by *rational* planning and 'collective control', by the use of scientific and technological advances, by the improvement of working conditions and, perhaps most important of all, by the reduction of working hours. So the answer Marx gives to the problem of types of work which offer little in the way of pleasure or creativity or sense of achievement is to minimize their extent. In other words, people will work fewer hours, in better conditions and with less expenditure of their energy. And, despite its nostalgia for the simplicities of a pre-industrial world, the image in the *German Ideology* of a life beyond the division of labour is relevant here. Why might unpleasant forms of labour not be shared more widely by moving beyond the division of labour which condemns one person to be a bricklayer, another to be a lawyer and a third to be farm labourer? Why could lawyers not spend part of their working week or month labouring on the land or on a building site? Why could a farm labourer or bricklayer not have something to contribute to the adjudication of legal disputes? After all, the law decides that they are good enough to sit on juries.

The realm of necessity does not, therefore, have to condemn certain people to a life of painful and tedious labour. But Marx also points to something beyond this realm of necessity: 'The true realm of freedom, the development of human powers as an end in itself, begins beyond it, though it can only flourish with this realm of necessity as its basis' (1981: 959). What will be the life of men and women in this new realm of freedom? In the *Economic and Philosophical Manuscripts* of 1844 there is a telling comment – the comment of a young man, a poet, a philosopher, a revolutionary. He is commenting on how political economy preaches thrift, self-denial, asceticism: 'its true ideal is the ascetic but rapacious skinflint and the ascetic but productive slave'. Its self-denial is, Marx says, 'the denial of life and of all human needs':

> The less you eat, drink, buy books, go to the theatre, go dancing, go drinking, think, love, theorize, sing, paint, fence, etc., the more you save and the greater will become that treasure which neither moths nor maggots can consume – your *capital*. The less you *are*, the less you give expression to your life, the more you *have*, the greater is your *alienated* life and the more you store up of your estranged life . . . So all passion and all activity are lost in *greed*. (1975: 361)

And so here we have it: for the young Marx the non-alienated life is passion and activity, to *be* rather than to *have*, to enjoy the sensual pleasures of life: to eat and to drink, to make love, to dance, to fence, to visit the theatre, to paint pictures and read books and think. A quarter of a century later in *Capital*, looking at all that the worker is deprived of in the contemporary workplace, Marx still valued these sensual, creative and social pleasures. 'The worker needs time to satisfy intellectual and social needs, and the extent and number of these is conditioned by the general cultural values.' He specifies the essential needs which require time free from labour: 'Time for education, for intellectual development, for the fulfilment of social functions, for social intercourse, for the free play of the vital forces of his body and his mind, even the rest time of Sunday . . .' (1976: 375).

STANDARDS OF LIVING

Surely this kind of critique of capitalism is now irrelevant? However pertinent to the world of Victorian industrial capitalism, Marx's criticisms of labour conditions and his projections of declining living standards surely has little to say to the world of the early twenty-first century? Here, at least, *Capital* can be demonstrated to be empirically wrong? Who could dispute that standards of living of the working class has risen steadily in the century and a half since Marx drafted *Capital*; that the working class now works fewer hours for more money and has a material standard of living beyond the dreams of their (our) grandparents? The realm of necessity is still with us, but the realm of freedom imagined by Marx is surely now an increasing reality as wider and wider sections of society have both time and money to participate in all kinds of creative and social pleasures? I want to pose a few questions to this kind of complacency.

First, a focus restricted to the rising living standards of the working-class of Western Europe and North America, omits the absolute immiseration of workers in other parts of the world. Tens of millions of squatters and slum-dwellers, deprived of the basic means of human subsistence, struggle for survival by casual labour in the vast shanty towns that ring the cities of the global South: Mumbai, Mexico City, Dhaka, Lagos, Cairo, Karachi, Kinshasa-Brazzaville, Cape Town, São Paolo, Shanghai and Delhi.

These are today part of a global working class that produces essential goods mainly for the European and North American markets. Many of the clothes worn by the Victorian middle-classes were produced in sweatshops and slums in London. Today they are produced in sweatshops in China or South-East Asia. The working class is no longer confined within national boundaries but is a global social class. Any critical investigation of the conditions of labour – including widespread child-labour – in contemporary capitalism must begin with this reality.[3] Enrique Dussel has talked of 'a complete rereading of Marx, with new eyes: as a Latin American, from the growing poverty of the peripheral world, the underdeveloped and exploited of capitalism at the end of the twentieth century'. And he adds: 'Marx is, in the periphery, today, more pertinent than in the England of the mid-nineteenth century'.[4]

Even if we look solely at the working class in advanced capitalist societies, some important questions can be asked which suggest that even here Marx is not quite irrelevant yet. We might accept that in absolute terms there has been some improvement in working-class living standards. However, since Marx wrote, labour's share of total social wealth has increased little, if at all. Capitalism is no more equal than it was in Victorian Britain. There are many indicators that it has become more unequal in recent decades. Furthermore, insofar as there has been any improvement in wage levels and working conditions these have come about as the result of long and painful struggles by trade unions and by labour movements and as the result of the election of socialist organizations of one kind or another to governments across Europe in the last century and a half. These improvements have not come about despite Marx, then, but *because* of socialist movements – movements which often owed something to his writing. Such advances as have been achieved have often been against bitter and continuing resistance on the part of organized capital. And far from rising living standards being the product of developing capitalism, the true relation of cause and effect is the reverse. In the pages of *Capital*, as we have seen, Marx investigated the campaigns of organized labour in England which succeeded in reducing the working day to a 'normal' length. This was not a result of progress or of economic development or of the social conscience of employers. His studies of the effects of the Victorian Factory Acts demonstrated the extent to which both the development and the use of new technologies were a response to the pressure on profits which these Acts exerted. Technological innovation was often stimulated by labour struggles against organized capital. Marx paid close attention to how these gains were relentlessly contested by capital. Such progress as there has been – whether in wages, working conditions, or hours of labour and free time – have always been temporary, contingent on the balance of political forces and thus liable to reversal. There is little doubt that the last quarter of a century has seen a profound defeat for organized labour across the developed world and in all kinds of way a reversal of many of the gains of the post-war period. So, for instance, Juliet Schor's studies of working time in the United States concluded that working hours were longer in the early 1990s than they had been 40 years previously and, if present trends continued, would have reached the levels of the 1920s by the beginning of this century.[5] Recent research on working time in Europe has tended to confirm that the long-term decline in working hours has been reversed in the last 20 years and that there is now a marked trend towards the both the lengthening and the intensification of working-time of wage labour.[6]

Further, we need to ask what exactly we mean by standard of living. Can this be measured by the ownership of cars and televisions per household, by the quantity of food consumed, by the flood of consumer goods purchased? For Marx what had to be confronted was the experience of work in modern industry and what this did to the human being. In narrowly material terms it produced physical injuries, exhaustion, sickness, even premature death. But look again at that classic statement of the immiseration thesis in *Capital* and the particular forms which it takes: 'the mass of misery, oppression, slavery, degradation and exploitation grows'. None of these terms are narrowly materialist. Here and throughout *Capital* there is stress on the mental and emotional damage of life under capitalism – on the deadening of the senses in noisy work environments, on the mind-numbing tedium of machine-minding, on the sheer futility experienced in hour after hour of performing repetitive tasks. This is a degradation of everything it means to be a human being. Every sense is damaged. Every creative potential is destroyed.

> Try putting 13 little pins in 13 little holes 60 times an hour, eight hours a day. Spot-weld 67 steel plates an hour, then find yourself one day facing a new assembly-line needing 110 an hour. Fit 100 coils to 100 cars every hour; tighten seven bolts three times a minute. Do your work in noise 'at the safety limit', in a fine mist of oil, solvent and metal dust. Negotiate for the right to take a piss – or relieve yourself furtively behind a big press so that you don't break the rhythm and lose your bonus. Speed up to gain the time to blow your nose or get a bit of grit out of your eye. Bolt your sandwich sitting in a pool of grease because the canteen is 10 minutes away and you've only got 40 for your lunch-break. As you cross the factory threshold, lose the freedom of opinion, the freedom of speech, the right to meet and associate supposedly guaranteed under the constitution. Obey without arguing, suffer punishment without the right of appeal, get the worst jobs if the manager doesn't like your face. Try being an assembly-line worker.[7]

This is Andre Gorz writing about factory workers in France in the early 1970s – and exhibiting precisely the experience of misery and oppression and slavery and degradation and exploitation which Marx referred to. The story was and remains the same for large numbers of working men and women from Lancashire cotton mills in the 1850s to factories, car plants, steelworks across the world, from China to Poland, from Mexico to Michigan, a century and a century and a half later. Nor is the situation that much different if we look at the working lives of tens of millions of red-eyed office workers, hunched over their computers in open-plan offices.

Generations of Western Marxists have bemoaned the incorporation of the working class into the political status quo and have obsessively worried at the question of ideology, as if the issue was primarily a matter of consciousness. But the endless bitter destructive war between capital and labour at the core of capitalism – the productive process – is mostly outside the purview of cultural materialism, media studies and Marxist studies of ideology. On the one side science and technology are utilized to make human labour as productive as possible, or, which is the same thing, to force the workers to work to the limit of their physical and psychological capabilities. There is only one purpose of these industrial enterprises and of these labour-saving devices: to make the largest possible profit whatever the cost to the physical and mental health of the producers. Their work must be externally imposed on them. Rebelling against the speed of production-lines, the shortness of rest periods, the petty tyranny of supervisors, the general tedious and mind-numbing futility of the job, resistance takes various forms: sabotage and breakages, absenteeism, walking out of work in mid-shift. Or, outside of the workplace, it becomes diverted into rage and violence, alcohol and drugs, gambling and stupid lotteries, competitive sport and terminal despair.

For Marx, the reign of freedom would begin when the material needs of all human beings were met – material needs which of course include not just the consumption of material goods but also a meaningful and creative life in which work is a positive activity. This moment, Sartre commented, was the point when Marx's thinking would at last become irrelevant: 'As soon as there will exist *for everyone* a margin of real freedom beyond the production of life, Marxism will have lived out its span; a philosophy of freedom will take its place.'[8] That day has not arrived yet. Whether it has been postponed indefinitely remains to be seen. Who knows what 'glorious Phantom' may yet 'Burst, to illumine our tempestuous day'?[9]

NOTES

1. INTRODUCTION: READING MARX

1 'One thing's for sure, I'm not a Marxist'. I want to acknowledge here some helpful discussions with several friends: Lena Andriakaina, Paul Bowman, Suman Gupta, Jenny Iles, Keith Nield and Peter Weston.
2 Stuart MacIntyre, *The Reds. The Communist Party of Australia from Origins to Illegality* (Sydney: George Allen & Unwin, 1998).
3 E. Olin Wright, 'Class Analysis, History and Emancipation', *New Left Review* I/202, (November–December 1993), 15–35. See also G. A. Cohen, 'Marxism after the Collapse of the Soviet Union', *The Journal of Ethics*, vol. 3, no. 2, (1999), 99–104.
4 See Stephen Cohen, *Failed Crusade. America and the Tragedy of Post-Communist Russia*, updated edition (New York: Norton 2001).
5 See Robert Service, *Comrades! A History of World Communism* (Cambridge, MA: Harvard University Press, 2007). The Communist Party of Great Britain never had anything like the membership and influence of the Italian and French parties. Membership was around 45,000 at the end of the war. By 1991, when the party was dissolved, it had fallen to less than 5,000.
6 Eric Hobsbawm, *Age of Extremes. The Short Twentieth Century 1914–1991* (London: Michael Joseph, 1994), p. 563.
7 Jacques Derrida, *Specters of Marx*, trans. Peggy Kamuf (New York: Routledge, 1994), p. 52.
8 *The Times*, 9 November 2008.
9 *Time Magazine,* vol. 173, no. 5, 2 February 2009.
10 Karl Marx and Frederick Engels, *The German Ideology*, Moscow: Progress Publishers, 1964; Karl Marx and Frederick Engels, *The German Ideology. Part One with Selections from Parts Two and Three . . .* , ed. C. J. Arthur, (London: Lawrence and Wishart, 1970).
11 The importance of the energy and commitment of Engels in getting so much of Marx's writing into print before his own death in 1895 is highlighted by the subsequent indifference of the German Social Democratic Party which had the rights to the literary remains (*Nachlass*) of Marx and Engels. Many of these writings remained unpublished and in manuscript form and some of Marx's key works

were allowed to fall out of print in the years before the First World War. There was no attempt to publish a complete edition of their writings before the 1920s. See Paul Thomas, 'Critical Reception: Marx Then and Now', *The Cambridge Companion to Marx*, ed. T. Carver (Cambridge: Cambridge University Press, 1991), pp. 23–54.

12 For what it's worth, I think the 99-year-old Menshevik Karl Marx would have given his support to Lenin's provisional government after the October Revolution. His disposition towards the contending groups at the apex of the Soviet state after the death of Lenin in 1924 is harder to imagine with any clarity. However, I think the recalcitrant old intellectual would have disappeared into one of Stalin's labour camps after 1936.

13 But see Barbara Taylor's critical comments in her important study *Eve and the New Jerusalem* (London: Virago, 1983), pp. xv–xvi, 284–5.

14 There is a large literature on this topic, including many empirical studies of female labour and domestic labour. Two useful starting places are: *Feminism and Materialism. Women and Modes of Production*, eds A. Kuhn and A-M. Wolpe (London: Routledge, 1978); Ben Fine, *Women's Employment and the Capitalist Family* (London: Routledge, 1992).

15 See the useful introduction of Michelle Phillips to Friedrich Engels, *The Origins of the Family, Private Property and the State* (Harmondsworth: Penguin, 1985).

16 S. S. Prawer, *Karl Marx and World Literature* (Oxford: Oxford University Press, 1978).

17 Quoted in *Karl Marx and Frederick Engels. On Literature and Art*, ed. L. Baxandall and S.Morawski (New York: International General, 1974), p. 15.

18 For an important study which surveys the work of such central figures as Lukacs, Bloch, Adorno, Marcuse and Sartre see Fredric Jameson, *Marxism and Form. Twentieth-Century Dialectical Theories of Literature* (Princeton: Princeton University Press, 1971).

19 Maurice Blanchot, 'Marx's Three Voices' (1968), in *Friendship*, trans. Elisabeth Rottenberg (Stanford: Stanford University Press, 1997), pp. 98–100.

2. POLITICS: THE 1848 REVOLUTIONS

1 As Sartre put it: 'The only way the intellectual can really distance himself from the official ideology decreed from above is by placing himself alongside those whose very existence contradicts it.' Jean-Paul Sartre, *Between Existentialism and Marxism* (London: Verso, 1983), p. 256.

2 See Georg Lukacs, *The Young Hegel. Studies in the Relations between Dialectics and Economics*, trans. R. Livingstone (London: Merlin Press, 1975).

3 See also Marx's speech to the Cologne Democratic Society, 4 August 1848, MECW 7: 556–7.

3. MATERIALIST HISTORIES

1 For a useful recent selection of Marx's journalism see: *Despatches for the New York Tribune: Selected Journalism of Karl Marx*, ed. James Ledbitter (Harmondsworth: Penguin, 2007).
2 'The Manchester School' was a common term in the 1840s and 1850s for the programme of radical free-trade policies associated with the Anti-Corn Law League which had its headquarters in Manchester.
3 The survival of aristocratic influence in Britain generated one of the liveliest debates among English Marxist historians of the 1960s. It was revived in the 1980s. See: Perry Anderson, 'Origins of the Present Crisis', first published in *New Left Review* 23 (1964), reprinted in *English Questions* (London: Verso, 1992); E. P.Thompson, 'The Peculiarities of the English', first published in *Socialist Register* (1965), reprinted in his *The Poverty of Theory and Other Essays* (London: Merlin, 1978). The debate is usefully summarized in Keith Nield, 'A Symptomatic Dispute? Notes on the Relation Between Marxian Theory and Historical Practice in Britain', *Social Research*, vol. 47, no. 3 (1980). For some international ramifications see D. Blackbourn and G. Eley, *The Peculiarities of German History. Bourgeois Society and Politics in Nineteenth-Century Germany* (Oxford: Oxford University Press, 1984). Perry Anderson returned to the topic in 1987 in a powerful essay, 'The Figures of Descent', reprinted in *English Questions* (London: Verso, 1992).
4 These were edited, expanded and published together by Engels in 1895 as *The Class Struggles in France: 1848–1850*.
5 Victor Hugo, *Napoleon the Little* (New York: Howard Fertig, 1992); Pierre-Joseph Proudhon, *La Révolution sociale demontrée par le coup d'état du 2 décembre 1851* [1852] (Paris: Rivière, 1936).
6 As he commented in a letter of 1871, on the unexpected combination of circumstances which gave rise the Paris Commune, history 'would be of a very mystical nature, if "accidents" played no part' (1975b: 248).
7 Marx is presumably alluding to a passage in Hegel's *Philosophy of History* about Caesar and the end of the Roman Republic:

> [I]t became immediately manifest that only a single will could guide the Roman state, and now the Romans were compelled to adopt that opinion; since in all periods of the world a political revolution is sanctioned in men's opinions, when it repeats itself. Thus, Napoleon was twice defeated, and the Bourbons twice expelled. By repetition that which at first appeared merely a matter of chance and contingency becomes a real and ratified existence. (G. W. F. Hegel, *The Philosophy of History*, trans. J. Sibree (New York: Dover, 1956), p. 312)

8 See here the important essay by Perry Anderson: 'The Notion of Bourgeois Revolution' in *English Questions* (London: Verso, 1992).
9 A useful introductory survey is provided in chapter 7 of Ernest Mandel, *The Formation of the Economic Thought of Karl Marx*

(New York: Monthly Review, 1971). For two important but often difficult studies: Roman Rosdolsky, *The Making of Marx's 'Capital'*, trans. P. Burgess (London: Pluto Press, 1976); Antonio Negri, *Marx Beyond Marx. Lessons on the 'Grundrisse'*, trans. H. Cleaver, M. Ryan and M. Viano (London: Pluto, 1991).

10 Karl Marx, *Precapitalist Economic Formations,* trans. Jack Cohen (London: Lawrence & Wishart, 1964). E. J. Hobsbawm's 'Introduction' is very useful.

11 Eric Hobsbawm usefully outlines major limitations in their historical knowledge (itself reflecting the limitations of their time): 'It was . . . thin on pre-history, on primitive communal societies and on pre-Columbian America, and virtually non-existent on Africa. It was not impressive on the ancient or medieval Middle East, but markedly better on certain parts of Asia, notably India, but not on Japan. It was good on classical antiquity and the European middle ages, though Marx's (and to a lesser extent Engels') interest in this period was uneven. It was, for the times, outstandingly good on the period of rising capitalism.' Ibid., p. 26.

12 Friedrich Engels, *The Origins of the Family, Private Property and the State*, ed. Michelle Phillips (Harmondsworth: Penguin, 1985), p. 214.

13 There is a substantial literature, mostly from the 1970s, on the Asiatic mode of production. A good place to start is Perry Anderson's long essay 'The "Asiatic Mode of Production"', appended to his *Lineages of the Absolutist State* (London: New Left Books, 1974).

14 L. Althusser and E. Balibar, *Reading Capital*, trans. B. Brewster (London: New Left Books, 1970), p. 202.

15 There is a famous poem by Brecht – 'Questions from a Worker who Reads' – which makes this point graphically and succinctly. Here are the opening three lines:

Who built Thebes of the seven gates?
In the books you will find the names of kings.
Did the kings haul up the lumps of rock?

16 Engels many years later described this tribute to the defeated Paris insurrection by Marx as 'one of his most powerful articles', 'Marx and the *Neue Rheinische Zeitung* (1848–49)' (1884), in MECW 26: 120.

17 Harvey Kaye, *The British Marxist Historians: An Introductory Analysis* (Oxford: Polity Press, 1984), is useful but sometimes tends towards hagiography and obscures some real differences among these historians. Other useful sources include: *Radical History Review* 19, 'Special Issue: Marxism and History: The British Contribution' (Winter 1978–9) and Bill Schwarz, 'The People in History: The Communist Party Historians' Group, 1946–56' in Richard Johnson (ed.) *Making Histories: Studies in History-Writing and Politics* (London: Hutchinson, 1982).

18 For an excellent example of the latter see Raphael Samuel, ed., *Miners, Quarrymen and Saltworkers* (London: Routledge, 1977).

19 E. P. Thompson, *The Making of the English Working Class*, 2nd edition (Harmondsworth: Penguin, 1968), p. 13.
20 George Rude, *Paris and London in the Eighteenth Century: Studies in Popular Protest* (London: Fontana, 1970), pp. 10–12.
21 Christopher Hill, *The World Turned Upside Down* (Harmondsworth: Penguin, 1975), pp. 363–4.
22 Christopher Hill, 'Historians on The Rise of British Capitalism', *Science and Society* 14 (1950), 321.
23 Jean-Paul Sartre, *Search for a Method* [1960], trans. Hazel Barnes (New York: Random House, 1968). Subsequent references are inserted in parentheses in the text.

4. POLITICAL ECONOMY AND THE HISTORY OF CAPITALISM

1 See Adam Smith, *An Inquiry Into the Nature and Causes of the Wealth of Nations* (1776) 2 vols, ed. R. H. Campbell and A. S. Skinner, Vol. II of *The Glasgow Edition of the Works and Correspondence of Adam Smith* (Indianapolis: Liberty Fund, 1981).
2 See Michael Levin, 'In Defense of Scrooge' (18 December 2000) at the webpage of the Ludwig von Mises Institute: http://mises.org/article.aspx?Id=573 (accessed 10 September 2009). This is probably not meant to be read ironically, though it is very funny if you do.
3 See Keith Wrightson, *Earthly Necessities. Economic Lives in Early Modern Britain, 1540–1750* (Harmondsworth: Penguin, 2002), pp. 10–13.
4 Peter Linebaugh, *The Magna Carta Manifesto. Liberties and Commons For All* (Berkeley: University of California Press, 2008), p. 14. Linebaugh's *The London Hanged. Crime and Civil Society in the Eighteenth Century*, 2nd edition (London: Verso, 2006) is an important contribution to any future understanding of 'primitive accumulation' and the economic and social transformations preceding industrialization and urban growth.
5 For an important study which takes some of these questions further see: Maurice Dobb, *Studies in the Development of Capitalism* (London: Routledge, 1963). First published in 1946 this book stimulated a wide-ranging debate among Marxists and historians. Major contributions were collected in *The Transition from Feudalism to Capitalism*, ed. R. H. Hilton (London: New Left Books, 1976).
6 Adam Smith, op.cit., pp. 13–14.
7 It is surprising that in his important studies of the institutions of disciplinary power in modern society Michel Foucault had so little to say about the factory or the workplace in general.
8 An enormous amount of important work has been done on these questions by historians. For some influential British studies: E. J. Hobsbawm, 'Custom, Wages and Work-load' in *Labouring Men* (London: Weidenfeld and Nicholson, 1964); E. P. Thompson, 'Time, Work-Discipline and Industrial Capitalism' in *Customs in Common* (London: Merlin, 1991); Raphael Samuel, 'Workshop of the

World: Steam Power and Hand Technology in Mid-Victorian Britain', *History Workshop Journal*, 3, Spring 1977.

5. THE POLITICS OF LABOUR

1 *Review of Reviews* (April 1893), 399.
2 H. Collins and C. Abramsky, *Karl Marx and the British Labour Movement: Years of the International* (London: Macmillan, 1965), pp. 61, 68–70, 82–3.
3 He had made a similar historical comparison in an article of 1853: 'We must not forget that strikes and combinations among the serfs were the hot-beds of the medieval communes, and that those communes have been in their turn, the source of life of the now ruling bourgeoisie' (1971: 190).
4 The case attracted public attention, see the accounts in *The Examiner* 26 June 1863 and *The Penny Illustrated Magazine*, 27 June 1863.
5 For a more or less Marxian reading of Magna Carta see Peter Linebaugh, *The Magna Carta Manifesto. Liberties and Commons for All* (Berkeley: California University Press, 2008).
6 Engels provides an extended critique of Malthus in his 'Outlines of a Critique of Political Economy', published by Marx in the *Deutsch-Französische Jahrbüche* in the spring of 1844. See MECW3: 418ff.
7 Especially useful here is *Marx and Engels on Malthus*, ed. R. L. Meek (London: Lawrence & Wishart, 1953).

6. REFORM AND REVOLUTION

1 Alfred Cobban, *A History of Modern France. Vol 3: 1871–1962* (Harmondsworth: Penguin, 1965), p. 23.
2 On the early development of the SPD see: Roger Morgan, *The German Social Democrats and the First International 1864–1872* (Cambridge: Cambridge University Press, 1965).
3 Marx's *Critique of the Gotha Programme* was a key reference point for Lenin's *State and Revolution* (1917).
4 This is one prediction that was to come true 40 years later. On the compromises of German Social Democracy during the German Revolution of 1918–19 a useful place to start is Richard N.Hunt, *German Social Democracy 1918–33* (New Haven: Yale University Press, 1964).
5 Marx makes the same point in volume 3 of *Capital* criticising notions of 'natural justice'. The justice of transaction between agents arises from the relations of production. Legal forms are, he says, merely forms of these relations: 'The content is just so long as it corresponds to the mode of production and is adequate to it. It is unjust as soon as it contradicts it. Slavery, on the basis of the capitalist mode of production, is unjust; so is cheating on the quality of commodities' (1981: 460–1).
6 Karl Marx, *Theories of Surplus Value*, vol. 2, trans. Renate Simpson (London: Lawrence & Wishart, 1969), pp. 117–18.

7 See in particular Roman Rosdolsky, *Engels and the "Nonhistoric" Peoples: the National Question in the Revolution of 1848*, ed. and trans. J-P. Himka (Glasgow: Critique Books, 1986).
8 See, for instance, Teodor Shanin, ed. *Late Marx and the Russian Road: Marx and the Peripheries of Capitalism* (New York: Monthly Review Press, 1983).

7. CONCLUSION: AFTER CAPITALISM

1 This powerful image of the relations between labour and art is explored in one of the great works of twentieth-century Marxism: Theodor Adorno and Max Horkheimer, *Dialectic of the Enlightenment* [1944], trans. J. Cumming (London: Verso, 1979), pp. 32ff.
2 The vital contribution of *Potere Operaio* (workers' power), *Autonomia* and theorists like Mario Tronti, Sergio Bologna, Antonio Negri, Franco Piperno, Oreste Scalzone, and Paolo Virno to a rereading of Marx on work is outlined in Steve Wright, *Storming Heaven: Class Composition and Struggle in Italian Autonomist Marxism* (London: Pluto, 2002).
3 See Mike Davis, *Planet of Slums* (London: Verso, 2006) for a grim picture of the appalling effects of neoliberal economic policies across the world. The Victorian sweatshop, the armies of half-starved casual labourers and the principles of classical political economy – the world in which Marx wrote *Capital* – is now to be found across the cities of what used to be called 'the Third World'.
4 Enrique Dussel, 'The Four Drafts of Capital: Toward a New Interpretation of the Dialectical Thought of Marx', *Rethinking Marxism*, vol. 13, no. 1 (Spring 2001), 10.
5 Juliet Schor, *The Overworked American. The Unexpected Decline of Leisure* (New York: Basic Books, 1992).
6 See Pietro Basso, *Modern Times, Ancient Hours: Working Lives in the Twenty-First Century* (London: Verso Books, 2003).
7 Michel Bosquet [Andre Gorz], 'The "Prison Factory"' *New Left Review* I/73, (May-June 1972), 23–34. No one has contributed more than Gorz to the rethinking of work and of what Marx might contribute to this. See, for instance, his *Farewell to the Working Class* (London: Pluto, 1982) and *Paths to Paradise. On the Liberation from Work* (London: Pluto, 1985).
8 Jean-Paul Sartre, *Search for a Method*, trans. H. Barnes (New York: Random House, 1963), p. 34.
9 The reference is to Shelley's magnificent political sonnet, as apposite in 2009:

England in 1819
An old, mad, blind, despis'd, and dying king,
Princes, the dregs of their dull race, who flow
Through public scorn – mud from a muddy spring,
Rulers who neither see, nor feel, nor know,

But leech-like to their fainting country cling,
Till they drop, blind in blood, without a blow,
A people starv'd and stabb'd in the untill'd field,
An army, which liberticide and prey
Makes as a two-edg'd sword to all who wield,
Golden and sanguine laws which tempt and slay,
Religion Christless, Godless – a book seal'd,
A Senate – Time's worst statute unrepeal'd,
Are graves, from which a glorious Phantom may
Burst, to illumine our tempestuous day.

Shelley was one of Marx's favourite poets of course.

FURTHER READING

The literature on Marx and Marxism is vast. The following details are here to provide suggestions for further reading and are restricted to what is easily available in English. There is a much longer bibliography in Tom Bottomore's *A Dictionary of Marxist Thought*, pp. 533–66.

WORKS BY MARX

Marx's major works are all now available in English translation. An English edition of the *Collected Works of Marx and Engels* has been published in fifty volumes by Lawrence and Wishart (London), International Publishers (New York) and Progress Publishers (Moscow), in collaboration with the Institute of Marxism-Leninism in Moscow. I should acknowledge permission from Lawrence and Wishart to quote from these volumes. This is gradually being made freely available online – with the additional value of being fully searchable – by the excellent Marx and Engels Internet Archive: (http://www.marxists.org/archive/marx/index.htm).

Perhaps the most useful edition of Marx available in English is the Pelican Marx Library, published in paperback by Penguin Books in association with *New Left Review*, under the general editorship of Quintin Hoare. It consists of new translations of three volumes of political writings, a single volume of the early writings, the massive *Grundrisse*, and all three volumes of *Capital*. Each of these is prefaced by a substantial introduction. I want to acknowledge permission from New Left Review to quote extensively from these eight volumes – and particularly from Marx's masterpiece, *Capital*, vol. 1.

There are many anthologies of extracts from Marx (and usually Engels too). I'd particularly recommend *Karl Marx: Selected Writings*, edited by David McLellan.

New readers shouldn't delay reading Marx until they have absorbed and understood some introductory guide or commentary. This would be a recipe for endless delay and uncertainty. The following are a few suggestions for places to start reading Marx:

Theses on Feuerbach (1845)
Here is the young Marx pronouncing in unusually succinct form his critique of philosophy. They are to be found in the Penguin *Early Writings*, edited by Colletti, and elsewhere.

The Eighteenth Brumaire of Louis Bonaparte
A wonderful piece of contemporary history. This is to be found in the Penguin *Surveys from Exile: Political Writings*, vol. 2, and elsewhere.

Capital, volume 1, chapter 1, section 4.
This is Marx's most influential discussion of 'commodity fetishism'.

Capital, volume 1, chapter 10.
This long chapter, 'The Working Day', is a sustained piece of argument, combining both the critique of political economy and a sharp political reading of contemporary history.

Capital, volume 1, chapter 25.
An extended account of the effects of technological change on labour. The third section is the most useful discussion of the reserve army of labour.

Capital, volume 1, chapter 27
On the dispossession of the peasantry and the creation of free labour – an important section of the longer account of 'so-called primitive accumulation'.

Critique of the Gotha Programme
The late Marx dealing with specific political issues. It is brief and to the point. This is to be found in the Penguin *Political Writings*, vol. 3, and elsewhere.

SECONDARY READING

General

Biography can provide some useful contexts for a critical reading of Marx's writings. Franz Mehring's biography, first published in German in 1918, is stolid but it was written by someone who knew Engels and the world of nineteenth-century German socialism. This gives it a certain authority and an eye for detail. Francis Wheen's recent *Karl Marx* is much more readable. Jerrold Seigel's *Marx's Fate* and David McLellan's *Karl Marx: His Life and Thought* are much more than biographies. Yvonne Kapp's biography of Eleanor Marx is a rich source for the life of the Marx family in London.

Of general commentaries on Marx there is never an end. Peter Osborne's *How to Read Marx* is an excellent recent introduction. Short and to the point, it provides thoughtful readings of a number of important extracts from Marx. Jon Elster's *Making Sense of Marx* is a formidable work of exposition and critical commentary. Allen Oakley's *The Making of Marx's Critical Theory* is a very handy guide to the actual texts of Marx. Anthony Brewer's *A Guide to Marx's Capital* is equally useful for navigating around this massive three-volume text. For three excellent studies – thorough, lucid and thoughtful – of specific themes running through Marx's work, see Simon Clarke's *Marx's Theory of Crisis*, Ali Rattansi's *Marx and the Division of Labour* and Geoffrey Kay's *The Economic Theory of the Working Class*.

1848

There is massive amount of discussion of Marx's formative period of writing in the 1840s. A useful place to start is the typically clear and concise account of David McLellan's *The Young Hegelians and Karl Marx*. His *Marx Before Marxism* is also worth looking at. Gareth Stedman Jones's book-length introduction to the recent (2002) Penguin edition of the *Communist Manifesto* is sometimes grumpy, but it is always lucid and concise. It presents a valuable overview of Marx's complex intellectual formation. Lucio Colletti's introduction to the Penguin *Early Writings* is brilliant. Several of the essays in Louis Althusser's *For Marx* open up valuable critical perspectives on the early works. Herbert Marcuse's *Reason and*

Revolution and Jean Hyppolite's *Studies on Marx and Hegel* are still worth going back to.

History and Political Economy

This topic has generated considerable discussion, though much of it pitched at the level of philosophy without much engagement with real histories. Gerry Cohen's *Karl Marx's Theory of History* has been influential and is at least clear and focused. Maurice Dobb's *Studies in the Development of Capitalism* was first published in 1946 but is still worth reading as an attempt to bring a critical political economy to bear on concrete historical material. For an example of a historian grappling with how to deploy Marx's concepts in concrete analysis see Gareth Stedman Jones's essay 'Class Struggle and Industrial Revolution' in his *Languages of Class*. Perry Anderson's *Arguments within English Marxism*, a fair-minded critique of Edward Thompson, demonstrates the political stakes of divergent appropriations of Marx in the 1960s and 70s.

For one of the most productive of modern readings of *Capital*, see Harry Braverman's *Labor and Monopoly Capitalism* – a seminal work on the labour process which generated a considerable literature in the 1970s. Moishe Postone's *Time, Labor and Social Domination* is one of the most original and challenging interpretations of the later Marx in recent years.

There are endless commentaries on Marx's theories of ideology. A good place to start is an excellent essay by Stuart Hall, 'The problem of ideology'. This points the way to further relevant reading. *Marxism and Literature*, by Raymond Williams is a major study of every aspect of Marx's work. The large volume *Marxism and the Interpretation of Culture* is a wonderful collection of essays and debates on a broad range of questions to do with ideology and culture. Janet Wolff's *The Social Production of Art* is an essential starting place for thinking about the implications of Marx's work for any understanding of the arts, though it ranges more widely than that. See also Margaret Rose, *Marx's Lost Aesthetic*.

Politics

There are several studies which explore relations between Marx's political theories and his political activities. Alan Gilbert's *Marx's*

Politics is useful, though it is mostly about the revolutions of 1848. His article 'Salvaging Marx from Avineri' ranges more widely. For two recent thought-provoking studies, which take opposing views of Marx's understanding of democracy, see August Nimtz's *Marx and Engels: Their Contribution to the Democratic Breakthrough* and Allan Megill's *Karl Marx: The Burden of Reason*. There is a massive literature on the history of nineteenth-century socialism. An important study, providing an essential context for any understanding of the political activities of Marx and Engels between the 1840s and the 1890s, is Geoff Eley, *Forging Democracy. The History of the Left in Europe 1850–2000*, especially Part 1, 'Making Democracy Social'.

Finally, for new work bringing Marx's categories to bear on some dimensions of the current conjuncture see Robert Brenner's *The Economics of Global Turbulence*, Andrew Glynn's, *Capitalism Unleashed*, Saad-Filho's *Anti-Capitalism: A Marxist Introduction*, Hardt and Negri's *Empire* and David Harvey's *A Brief History of Neoliberalism*.

SELECT BIBLIOGRAPHY

PRINCIPAL WRITINGS IN ENGLISH

Marx

Early Writings, trans R. Livingstone and G. Benton, London: Penguin, 1975.
Revolutions of 1848, Political Writings, vol. 1, ed. D. Fernbach, London: Penguin, 1973.
Surveys from Exile, Political Writings, vol. 2, ed. D. Fernbach, London: Penguin, 1973.
Grundrisse. Foundations of the Critique of Political Economy (Rough Draft), trans. M. Nicolaus, London: Penguin, 1973.
A Contribution to the Critique of Political Economy, ed. M. Dobb, trans. S.Ryazanskaya, London: Lawrence & Wishart, 1969.
Capital. A Critique of Political Economy, vol. 1, intro. E. Mandel, trans. B. Fowkes, London: Penguin, 1976.
Capital. A Critique of Political Economy, vol. 2, intro. E. Mandel, trans. D. Fernbach, London: Penguin, 1978.
Capital. A Critique of Political Economy, vol. 3, intro. E. Mandel, trans. D. Fernbach, London: Penguin, 1981.
Precapitalist Economic Formations, trans. Jack Cohen, London: Lawrence & Wishart, 1964.
Theories of Surplus Value, 2 vols, trans. Emile Burns and Renate Simpson, London: Lawrence & Wishart, 1969.
Karl Marx: Selected Writings, edited by David McLellan, Oxford: Oxford University Press, 1977.

Marx and Engels

Collected Works, 50 volumes, London: Lawrence & Wishart, 1975–2000.
The German Ideology. Part One with selections from Parts Two and Three . . . ed. C. J. Arthur, London: Lawrence & Wishart, 1970.
Articles on Britain, Moscow: Progress Publishers, 1971.
Selected Correspondence, third revised edition, Moscow: Progress Publishers, 1975.

Engels

Ludwig Feuerbach and the End of Classical German Philosophy, Moscow: Progress Publishers, 1946.

SECONDARY WORKS

Althusser, L., *For Marx*, trans. B.Brewster, London: Verso, 1970.

Althusser L. and E. Balibar, *Reading Capital*, trans. B. Brewster, London: Verso, 1970.

Anderson, P., *Considerations on Western Marxism*, London: Verso, 1976.

—, *Arguments within English Marxism*, London: Verso, 1980.

Avineri, S., *Karl Marx on Colonialism and Modernisation*, New York: Anchor Books, 1969.

Bottomore, T., ed., *A Dictionary of Marxist Thought*, Oxford: Blackwell, 1983.

Braverman, H., *Labor and Monopoly Capitalism*, New York: Monthly Review Press, 1974.

Breckman, W., *Marx, the Young Hegelians, and the Origins of Radical Social Thought: Dethroning the Self*, Cambridge: Cambridge University Press, 1999.

Brenner, R., *The Economics of Global Turbulence*, London: Verso, 2006.

Brewer, A., *A Guide to Marx's Capital*, Cambridge: Cambridge University Press, 1984.

—, *Marxist theories of Imperialism. A Critical Survey*, 2nd edition, London: Routledge, 1990.

Carver, T., *The Post-Modern Marx*, Manchester: Manchester University Press, 1998.

Carver, T., ed., *Karl Marx: Texts on Method*, Oxford: Basil Blackwell, 1975.

—, *The Cambridge Companion to Marx*, New York: Cambridge University Press, 1991.

Clarke, S., *Marx's Theory of Crisis*, London: Macmillan, 1994.

Cohen, G. A., *Karl Marx's Theory of History. A Defence*, 2nd edition, Oxford: Oxford University Press, 2001.

Collins, H. and C. Abramsky, *Karl Marx and the British Labour Movement: Years of the International*, London: Macmillian, 1965.

Dobb, M., *Studies in the Development of Capitalism*, London: Routledge & Kegan Paul, 1963.

Eley, G., *Forging Democracy. The History of the Left in Europe 1850–2000*, Oxford: Oxford University Press, 2002.

Elster, J., *Making Sense of Marx*, Cambridge: Cambridge University Press, 1985.

Fine, B., *Marx's Capital*, 3rd edition, London: Macmillan, 1989.

Furet, F., *Marx and the French Revolution*, Chicago: Chicago University Press, 1988.

Gilbert, A., *Marx's Politics. Communists and Citizens*, Oxford: Martin Robertson, 1981.

Gilbert, A, 'Salvaging Marx from Avineri', *Political Theory*, vol. 4, no. 1 (February, 1976), 9–34.

Gorz, A., *Farewell to the Working Class: An Essay on Post-Industrial Socialism*, trans. Michael Sonenscher, London: Pluto Press, 1982.

Hall, S., 'The problem of ideology. Marxism without guarantees', *Marx: 100 Years On*, ed. B.Matthews, London: Lawrence & Wishart, 1983.

Hardt, M and A.Negri, *Empire*, Cambridge: Harvard University Press, 2000.

Harvey, D., *Consciousness and the Urban Experience. Studies in the History and Theory of Capitalist Urbanization*, Oxford: Basil Blackwell, 1985.

—, *A Brief History of Neoliberalism,* Oxford: Oxford University Press, 2006.

Hilton, R., ed., *The Transition from Feudalism to Capitalism*, London: New Left Books, 1976. (An expanded version of *The Transition from Feudalism to Capitalism: A Symposium*, New York: Science and Society edition, 1954.)

Hyppolite, J., *Studies on Marx and Hegel,* New York: Basic Books, 1969.

Kapp, Y., *Eleanor Marx,* vol. 1, London: Lawrence & Wishart, 1972.

Kay, G., *The Economic Theory of the Working Class*, London: Macmillan, 1979.

Korsch, K., *Marxism and Philosophy,* London: New Left Books, 1970.

Lenin, V.I., *The Development of Capitalism in Russia*, *Collected Works*, vol. 3, Moscow: Progress Publishers, 1960.

Lukacs, G., *History and Class Consciousness*, trans. Rodney Livingstone, London: Merlin, 1971.

—, *The Young Hegel: Studies in the Relations between Dialectics and Economics,* trans. Rodney Livingstone, Cambridge, MA: MIT Press, 1976.

Luxemburg, R., *The Russian Revolution and Leninism or Marxism?* Ann Arbor: University of Michigan Press, 1962.

MacKenzie, D., 'Marx and the Machine', *Technology and Culture*, vol. 25, no. 3. (July 1984), 473–502.

McLellan, D., *The Young Hegelians and Karl Marx*, New York: Praeger, 1969.

—, *Karl Marx: His Life and Thought,* London: Macmillan, 1973.

—, *Marx Before Marxism*, 2nd edition, London: Macmillan, 1980.

Mandel, E., *The Formation of the Economic Thought of Karl Marx*, New York: Monthly Review, 1971.

Marcuse, H., *Reason and Revolution. Hegel and the Rise of Social Theory*, 2nd edition, London: Routledge, 1955.

—, *Soviet Marxism. A Critical Analysis*, Harmondsworth: Penguin, 1971.

Megill, A., *Karl Marx: The Burden of Reason (Why Marx Rejected Politics and the Market),* Lanham: Rowman and Littlefield, 2002.

Negri, A., *Marx Beyond Marx: Lessons on the Grundrisse,* Brooklyn: Autonomedia, 1991.

Nelson, C. and Grossberg, L., eds, *Marxism and the Interpretation of Culture*, London: Macmillan, 1988.

Nimtz, A., *Marx and Engels: Their Contribution to the Democratic Breakthrough*, Albany: State University of New York Press, 2000.
Oakley, A., *The Making of Marx's Critical Theory. A Bibliographical Analysis*, London: Routledge & Kegan Paul, 1983.
Osborne, P., *How to Read Marx*, London: Granta, 2005.
Postone, M., *Time, Labor and Social Domination: A Reinterpretation of Marx's Critical Theory*, Cambridge: Cambridge University Press, 1996.
Rattansi, A., *Marx and the Division of Labour*, London: Macmillan, 1982.
Rigby, S. H., *Marxism and History. A Critical Introduction*, Manchester: Manchester University Press, 1987.
Roemer, J., *Free To Lose: An Introduction to Marxist Economic Philosophy*, Cambridge, MA: Harvard University Press, 1988.
Rosdolsky, R., *The Making of Marx's 'Capital'*, trans. P. Burgess, London: Pluto Press, 1976.
Rose, M., *Marx's Lost Aesthetic: Karl Marx and the Visual Arts*, Cambridge: Cambridge University Press, 1984.
Rowthorn, R., *Capitalism, Conflict and Inflation*, London: Lawrence & Wishart, 1980.
Saad-Filho, A., *The Value of Marx: Political Economy for Contemporary Capitalism*, London: Routledge, 2002.
—, *Anti-Capitalism: A Marxist Introduction*, London: Pluto, 2003.
Sartre, J-P., *Search for a Method*, trans. H. E. Barnes, New York: Vintage Books, 1968.
—, *Critique of Dialectical Reason: Volume One: Theory of Practical Ensembles*, trans. A. Sheridan-Smith, London: Verso, revised edition, 1991; *Volume Two (Unfinished): The Intelligibility of History*, ed. A.Elkaim-Sartre, trans. Q. Hoare, London: Verso, 1991.
Seigel, J., *Marx's Fate: The Shape of a Life*, 2nd edition, University Park: Pennsylvania State University Press, 1993.
Shaw, W. H., *Marx's Theory of History*, London: Hutchinson, 1978.
Ste Croix, G.de, *The Class Struggle in the Ancient Greek World*, London: Duckworth, 1982.
Stedman Jones, G., *Languages of Class. Studies in English working-class history, 1832–1982*, Cambridge: Cambridge University Press, 1985.
Sweezy, P., *The Theory of Capitalist Development*, 2nd edition, New York: Monthly Review Press, 1970.
Thomas, P., *Karl Marx and the Anarchists*, London: Routledge &. Kegan Paul, 1985.
Thompson, E. P., *The Making of the English Working Class*, 2nd edition, Harmondsworth: Penguin, 1968.
Warren, B., *Imperialism, Pioneer of Capitalism*, London: New Left Books, 1980.
Wheen, F., *Karl Marx*, London: Fourth Estate, 1999.
Wickham, C., ed., *Marxist History-writing for the Twenty-first Century*, Oxford: Oxford University Press for the British Academy, 2007.
Williams, R., *Marxism and Literature*, Oxford: Oxford University Press, 1977.

Wolff, J., *The Social Production of Art*, 2nd edition, London: Macmillan, 1991.

Wolff, R. P., *Understanding Marx: A Reconstruction and Critique of Capital,* Princeton: Princeton University Press, 1984.

INDEX